EAST END YOUTH MINISTRY 1880-1957

A Case Study in Urban Youth Ministry

Rev Dr Steve Griffiths

EAST END YOUTH MINISTRY 1880-1957

A Case Study in Urban Youth Ministry

YTC Press

YTC Press

An imprint dedicated to research on Youth, Theology & Culture

First published in 2007 by

YTC Press

– A Division of Youth Focus –

www.youthfocus.biz

ISBN: 978-1-84753-849-9

Youth Focus

Youth Focus is a partnership dedicated to providing good quality resources for those involved in Christian youth ministry at an affordable price. We undertake this ministry by

- Training volunteer, part-time and full-time youth workers throughout the world through our accredited online Emerge Academy, www.emergeacademy.net
- Providing lecture resources (scripts, handouts and PowerPoint presentations) for those involved in teaching youth ministry and associated disciplines, www.youthfocus.biz
- Publishing books, with our YTC Imprint through www.lulu.com, on youth ministry, ecclesiology, cultural studies, theology, education and associated disciplines

Youth Focus is based in the UK but partners with organisations around the world.

For more information, please contact Steve Griffiths through steve@youthfocus.biz or go to the websites:

www.youthfocus.biz
www.emergeacademy.net

This work is dedicated to the parishioners of St. Paul's, Stratford, East London through whom I developed a love and passion for urban youth ministry

It is also dedicated to Dr Pete Ward who has encouraged me constantly during my time studying at King's College, London and afterwards

Special thanks go to Jo, Scott, Lee and Rebekah – my constant inspirations

Contents

Acknowledgements

This book grew out of my ministry as Minister of St. Paul's, Stratford in East London and as Area Youth Officer for the Barking Episcopal Area. During my time working with Rt. Revd. Roger Sainsbury, I was privileged to get a glimpse into the rich heritage of youth ministry in the East End of London. I will always remain profoundly grateful to Bishop Roger for affording me that possibility.

During that time, I studied under Dr Pete Ward at King's College, London. This book forms part of the fruit of the research I undertook during my time there. I am grateful to Pete for his constant encouragement and his unerring critique of my ideas.

Introduction

The history and development of Christian urban youth ministry in Britain is both long and complex. Efforts to discern a moment of origin have been, and will always be, fruitless. All that can ever be discerned with any clarity are moments of critical development, not the moment of birth. To suggest that such work began with the social activism of, say, Dr. Barnardo, would do an injustice to, say, the tailor Thomas Cranfield who started nineteen Sunday, night and juvenile schools in London before his death in 1838. It might be possible to credit the urban youth ministry initiative to the 1802 Instructive Institution, founded in the Minories near the Tower of London for fifteen poor children. However, that would be to do an injustice to conscientious Reformed ministers such as Thomas Brooks who, one hundred and fifty years earlier (and less than half a mile away from The Minories), had produced his superb *Apples of Gold* treatise for young parishioners.[1] Perhaps some evangelically minded parents in eighth-century London created a prototype Sunday School for their children, the records of which have been lost in the mists of time! Sadly, we shall never know. Searching for origins is, frankly, pointless. To examine moments of critical development, however, is a more fruitful occupation. The reality is that these moments in the *modus procedendi* of Christian youth ministry - often lasting a generation or more - have usually coincided with paradigm shifts in ecclesiological development. If Ward's thesis in *Growing Up Evangelical* is to be believed, ecclesiological paradigm shifts are in no small part *attributable* to youth ministry developments. Writing of the evangelical constituency in particular, but with a thesis that probably transcends churchmanship, Ward rationalised that, "In an English context there is a good deal of agreement that modern-day evangelicalism has emerged as a powerful force within the Church and that this resurgence is in no small way due to the efforts of those engaged in work among young people and students."[2]

This book aims to examine one critical moment in the history and development of Christian urban youth ministry. Admittedly, the 'moment' under examination is both demographically particular (East London) and horologically extensive (1880-1957). Nevertheless, it is a 'moment' worth specific consideration for a number of reasons.

First, this was a period of extraordinary transition for London and the young people who inhabited its streets. Many works have been produced on the history of England's capital city during this period and it is not our aim to duplicate that material in any detail. Nevertheless, we briefly note, by way of introduction, the changing face of London during this era. In *Outcast London*, Stedman Jones commented that, "Between 1821 and 1851 [London's population] almost doubled; by the end of the century it had almost doubled again."[3] Such a population explosion inevitably altered the character and needs of the city. The first half of the twentieth-century provided no less an extraordinary rate of change. The growth of railways, commerce and industry; increasing ethnic diversity; the devastating effects of two World Wars; the development of the Welfare State; the expansion of educational opportunities – all these and more had a phenomenal impact on the inhabitants of London in general and the youth population in particular.

Yet this thesis is more specific still in examining just one part of London: namely, the East End. Its peculiar character, often caricatured by the Cockney spirit, the propensity for humour and song, and the quasi-historical invention of such people as Fagin and the Artful Dodger, is well known. Indeed, as Asa Briggs has commented, it was "During the 1880s and 1890s the term 'East End' began to be used generally: it suggested a different world, an unknown world, within the same city."[4] This was also a contemporary understanding, as Henry Mayhew's 1861 *London Labour and the London Poor* revealed: "In passing from the skilled operative of the West-end, to the unskilled workman of the Eastern quarter of London, the moral and intellectual change is so great, that it seems as if we were in a new land, and among another race."[5] But as O'Neill astutely recognised, "there is a difficulty in defining what and where the East End is, begins and ends. The physical East End is as difficult to define as the spiritual ideal with which so many cockneys, wherever they now live, feel such connection."[6] For our purposes, we take the western edge as being the City of London – boundaries dating back to the thirteenth-century – and its eastern edge as being that slightly hazy geographical area designated 'London over the Border', ending at Beckton. In terms of the River Thames, East London lies between St. Katherine's Dock and Beckton Gas Works.

Within that geographical boundary, we will examine the remarkable emphasis placed on youth ministry during our period. George Lansbury commented in *Looking Backwards and Forwards* that the East End enjoyed an "unreasonable and unexpected happiness in the middle of sordid conditions."[7] It is for others to assess the full reasons behind this optimism. One important factor, though, was the development of creative and courageous youth ministry. Dr. Thomas J. Barnardo, whose work amongst the poor and destitute children of the Stepney and Whitechapel districts has been well chronicled, is one example of this.[8] Brewery heir Frederick Charrington[9] and Salvation Army founder William Booth[10] were also successful practitioners. However, of more direct relevance to our own study is the development of four particular forms of Christian youth ministry: the Settlement movement, the formation of Boys' Clubs, parochial ministry and Public School Missions. Given the massive importance of such ministries in shaping the character, not only of individuals, but also of a city, surprisingly little research has been carried out in this area. It is half a century since the publication of McG. Eagar's notable work, *Making Men.*[11] Not since that time has there been a serious grappling with the vast wealth of primary material available.

Given the brevity of this book, it is possible to cast only a cursory glance at the wider context of the development of this youth ministry. For that reason, the bulk of the work will be an examination of a specific case study: namely, Dockland Settlement No.1. This fascinating youth project is most worthy of individual consideration. It touched the lives of literally thousands of young people. The youth ministry carried out there was ahead of its time in many ways. It became a model of good practice for many others to follow. It spawned a series of sister projects, not just in London, but throughout the South of England. Its demise was not the end of the story but merely the transition to a new chapter in becoming the famed and feted Mayflower Family Centre under the guidance of Reverend David Sheppard (later Bishop of Liverpool and Lord Liverpool).

We are not claiming that Dockland Settlement No. 1 is representative of urban youth ministry *in its totality* during the period in question. It is, at the most, representative of *one style* of urban youthwork. The lessons to be learnt from it will not be universal. The truth is - and many who have historical links do not wish to acknowledge this - that Dockland Settlement No.1 (and the Mayflower Family Centre which evolved out of this work) is, and always has been, an immensely privileged work. It has millions of pounds worth of plant. It has received millions of pounds of grant-aid. It has, since its inception, enjoyed the active patronage of royalty, peers, celebrities and famous clergymen. The young people who attended its clubs have enjoyed annual holidays to Belgium, France, Italy and Spain as well as numerous camps and weekend breaks in England. Part-time leaders had housing purchased for them in the locality. Since its inception, all full-time staff have enjoyed the luxury of Sabbatical breaks on a very regular basis, lasting from four months to, in a couple of cases, nearly a year. The list of privileges goes on and on. There are no other churches in the East End of London sharing that history. There are probably few throughout Britain. Nevertheless, it is worth studying both for its fascinating history and the massive impact it made.

Dockland Settlement No.1 developed in a dual context: specifically, a local context, in response to local needs, and a national context within a wider nineteenth- and early-twentieth-century religious movement of evangelical social action. Previous research and critique of the history of both Dockland Settlement No.1 and the Mayflower

Family Centre has been much the poorer for ignoring the fundamental importance of this dual context. In his book, *A Different Kind of Church*,[12] Watherston barely commented on the wider national context, an oversight that distorted the ensuing text. Similarly, the anecdotal nature of Settlement founder Kennedy-Cox's *An Autobiography*[13] did little to provide analysis of either the local situation or the influence of the wider Christian social movement of the times. To be fair to both authors, such analysis would have fallen outside the intent of their works. That does mean, however, that there is still the need for a contextual approach. It is hoped that this book will provide just that.

An appropriate and clear methodology in historical enquiry is vital if we are not to fall into the trap of merely 're-telling the tale'. There are as many methodological approaches as there are historians. However, the underlying approach to this work is that endorsed by other urban historians such as S.G. Checkland, who had this to offer in *The Study of Urban History*: "Some historians think mainly about secular trend, some about themes, and some about context…I think that we have learned by now that to be effective at any one of these three levels you must do some thinking about the other two."[14] This particular work aims to focus equally on trend, theme and context. This will be reflected in the chapter divisions and will provide a definite framework for what follows.

As with any academic endeavour, secondary sources have provided much information and support for the thesis. However, it is to be noted that this work is heavily reliant on primary material. To date, there has been no consideration of Dockland Settlement No.1, or the wider youth work in Canning Town, that has extensively drawn on archive material. All that has been written to date has been anecdotal history. As interesting – and vital – as this is, a more objective approach has been long overdue. It is hoped that such an approach will be found here. In developing this thesis, the current Mayflower Council gave me the privilege of unlimited access to all records and confidential memoranda. Further, I was able to explore the archives of St. Luke's, Victoria Dock as well as other archive sources that would inform the content and context of this work: those held at the Lambeth Palace library, Barnardo's archives, microfiches of the *Church Times* and *Church of England Newspaper*, census information and other local demographic material held at Newham Borough Council, historical records from Malvern College and Oxford University, archives from St. Cedd's, Canning Town and St. Paul's, Stratford New Town and records from the Church of England Diocese of Chelmsford.[15] In addition, a great deal of information was gleaned from the extensive round of interviews and conversations I had with those most intimately involved with the history and development of the youth work in Canning Town during this period. These individuals are credited in *Bibliography and Sources*, so need not be named here.

This book is not just the re-telling of a familiar story. It is breaking new ground in the research of urban youth ministry history. However, in breaking this new ground, we are mindful of Checkland's words that, "there is a resistance amongst [historians] to the idea that urban history should become a separate study, and even more strongly, to the notion that a further sub-division should develop so that there would appear scholars labelled as urban social historians, urban economic historians, and so on. This would certainly be to go too far."[16] Concurring with that view, we would not wish to create for ourselves the category of urban youth historian. Nevertheless, there is vital research to be done in this particular arena: not just so that we know where we have come from but so that we can better assess where we are heading.

There are some parts of the thesis that are highly contentious. It will undoubtedly provide a very real challenge; not just for those still involved in Mayflower ministry but for the wider evangelical constituency that has supported the work for so many years. However, it is our hope that engagement with this period of history will be an encouragement to both youth work practitioners in the East End of London and historians who wish to develop this most vital area of knowledge.

NOTES

[1] T. Brooks, *Apples of Gold*, 1660, in *The Works of Thomas Brooks*, (Edinburgh: Banner of Truth, 1980), I.171f.

[2] P. Ward, *Growing Up Evangelical* (London: SPCK, 1996), p.6

[3] G. Stedman Jones, *Outcast London*, (Oxford: Clarendon, 1971), p.160

[4] A. Briggs, *Victorian Cities*, (Harmondsworth: Pelican, 1968), p.314

[5] H. Mayhew, *London Labour and the London Poor*, 1861 (vol. 3, p.233) cited by Stedman Jones, *Outcast London*, p.30

[6] G. O'Neill, *My East End*, (Harmondsworth: Penguin, 1999), p.xviii

[7] Cited by Briggs, *Victorian Cities*, p.316

[8] For example, see A.E. Williams, *Barnardo of Stepney* (London: Allen & Unwin, 1966); J. Powell, *The Man Who Didn't Go to China*, (London: Lutterworth, 1947) and G. Wagner, *Barnardo* (London: Weidenfeld & Nicolson, 1979)

[9] See G. Thorne, *The Great Acceptance: The Life Story of F.N. Charrington*, (London: Hodder & Stoughton, 1913)

[10] See R. Hattersley, *Blood and Fire: The Story of William and Catherine Booth and their Salvation Army*, (London: Little, Brown, 1999) and G. Hanks, *God's Special Army: The Story of William Booth*, (Exeter: Religious Education Press, 1980)

[11] W. McG. Eagar, *Making Men*, (London: University of London, 1953)

[12] P. Watherston, *A Different Kind of Church*, (London: Marshall Pickering, 1994)

[13] R. Kennedy-Cox, *An Autobiography*, (London: Hodder & Stoughton, 1931)

[14] S.G. Checkland, in *The Study of Urban History*, (ed. H.J. Dyos, London: Edward Arnold, 1968), p.346

[15] In the course of this research I have studied literally hundreds of primary documents, newspapers and microfiches. For the sake of brevity, however, only those referred to in the text have been listed under *Bibliography and Sources*

[16] Checkland in *The Study of Urban History*, p.344

Chapter One

East London and Philanthropic Spirituality

Sociological development in the late-Victorian urban context has not suffered from a lack of analysis. Historians, economists, sociologists, theologians, political activists and even revisionists - chronicling every aspect of city life during that period - have produced a vast array of literature. It is not our intention to duplicate that work here. Should the reader wish to become better acquainted with pen-portraits, facts and figures of the squalid reality of urban living in the late-Victorian era, they should look elsewhere.[1] Rather, the purpose of this chapter is to explore that urban context specifically, and only, as a means of providing adequate context for the theme of our study. First, consideration will be given to the harsh reality of daily existence in East London, focussing especially on the late-Victorian period. Second, consideration will be given to the response of philanthropic activists to these horrendous conditions. Finally, conclusions will be drawn concerning what motivated these activists, the nature of their spirituality and to what extent their ministry proved effective. Having developed this *contextual* setting, we will be better able to explore the *trend* of youth ministry that evolved from this period before moving on, in the second part of this book, to our specific *theme*, which is the youth ministry carried out at Dockland Settlement No.1.

The East London Victorian Context

From the 1840s onwards, due primarily to the increase in centrally located industry and manufacturing, the City of London was de-populating at a quite extraordinary rate. Coupled with the dramatic rise in the London population as a whole, this inevitably created what Stedman Jones described as "pockets of intense poverty."[2] The East End suffered the most intense poverty of all as workers and casual labourers streamed into the area, seeking personal benefit from the industries that were growing up alongside the newly formed Dock and Railway initiatives.[3] By the beginning of our period, the situation was becoming acute. In the 1890s, for example, the population of inner East London rose by some 3.5%,[4] mainly as a result of increasing Jewish settlement, which, it was reckoned by Llewellyn Smith, had alone accounted for some 20,000 persons the previous decade.[5] However, the Borough of West Ham, the primary geographical area under concern in this work, experienced an even greater influx. Even as early as 1881, only 30% of the population of West Ham had been born in London.[6] As we shall see below, that situation was to become more acute still in the ensuing decades.

The intensity of poverty was difficult to measure. A number of audits attempted the task and both Andrew Mearns' 1883 *The Bitter Cry of Outcast London* and General Booth's 1890 *In Darkest England and the Way Out* were excellent attempts. However, it was left to Charles Booth to carry out the most extensive sociological audit of late-nineteenth century London. Work began on 10 September 1886 and, over the following seventeen-years, an equal number of volumes were produced for his work entitled *Life and Labour of the People of London.*[7] His statistical analysis was generally regarded as the most comprehensive work of the period and helped to inform and guide philanthropic strategy prior to the First World War. Inevitably though, statistics could not accurately portray the hideous intensity of the effects of poverty. Eyewitness accounts, such as that of Longstaff writing of "the narrow chest, the pale face, the weak eyes, the bad teeth, of the town-bred child",[8] were far more powerful. It was reading accounts of unimaginable human misery that led philanthropic activists to show initial interest in the East End districts. Upon entering the area, their eyes were opened to a world they could scarcely have imagined.

Poor housing and the lack of decent sanitation was a primary problem from which most other social evils stemmed.[9] Overcrowding was common, it being usual for between six and nine people to occupy a room. On occasions, room occupancy was found to be as high as fourteen individuals.[10] But as Dyos commented, slum housing and overcrowding was an inevitable cost of industrial expansion: "Slums were necessary so as not to dissipate too many resources in housing, and…while labour was abundant, cheap and docile, this was economically justifiable. The logic of this, tacitly accepted at the time, is that the slums helped to underpin Victorian prosperity…One of the real costs of industrial expansion was the making of slums."[11]

Stedman Jones has noted this lack of engagement with the harsh reality of slum dwelling: "Throughout the 1890s, there was a general lull in public concern about the condition of the very poor. Discussion of problems of poverty and degeneration was largely confined to experts, or to marginal political groupings like the Fabians."[12] This attitude can only be understood when we note that, "The traditional distinction between deserving and undeserving poor remained a central tenet of middle-class social philosophy both in its individualistic and in its collectivistic forms."[13] It was not so much lack of compassion that perpetuated the cruelty of East End poverty. Rather, it was a philosophical and political mind-set that, if not created by, was certainly enhanced by contemporary Darwinian extrapolation into the field of social science.

Hand in hand with the lack of social engagement went the very real fear, held by many, of the working-class element in East London. Since the collapse of the Thames shipbuilding industry in the mid-1860s, the East End had come to be seen as "a nursery of destitute poverty and thriftless, demoralized pauperism, as a community cast adrift from the salutary presence and leadership of men of wealth and culture, and as a potential threat to the riches and civilization of London and the Empire."[14] Perhaps the unemployment riots in February 1886 – resulting from the lowest temperatures recorded for thirty years – fuelled these fears. However, when civil strife and revolutionary activity failed to materialise during the great Dock Strike later that year, the perception of a brutal underclass able to hold the city to ransom was shown to be unfounded. Thereafter, as Stedman Jones commented, they were viewed with pity, "a small and hopeless remnant, a nuisance to administrators rather than a threat to civilization."[15]

This view, albeit revised, was still held largely from a distance. Few ventured into areas where casual labourers were struggling to provide for their family with daily, even hourly, pay.[16] Few outsiders could comprehend a hand to mouth existence where there was no incentive to save, no possibility of purchasing anything beyond the barest essentials of life, where life itself hung by a thread due to the serious medical conditions that raged throughout East End districts. It was only after the liminoid experience of the First World War, in which the gentleman and the docker were forced to develop mutual trust and understanding to survive trench warfare, that a wider understanding began to develop. Until then, however, the lot of the poor would remain a mystery to all but the most courageous few who dared to enquire further.

Those who did step into this strange world recognised almost immediately that, at the very heart of the tragedy of East End poverty, was the experience of young people. Concurring with Gerali's comment that "Only in the last century has there been the emergence of an adolescent subculture by name,"[17] we acknowledge that it is sometimes difficult to differentiate between the lot of the young person and adults at the end of the nineteenth-century. Nevertheless, statistical and other historical data provides a compelling picture of a group of people struggling and suffering, not least due to the economic burden they were expected to carry for their younger siblings and ageing parents.

In the first part of the nineteenth-century, silk weaving, sugar baking and shipbuilding had been the largest East End industries. Between 1830 and 1870, as these industries collapsed, a vacuum was created that would later be filled by the docks and the railways and associated industries. However, an agricultural depression in the 1880s forced rural labourers into the East End to seek employment, causing an even greater strain on this already struggling area of London. The resultant labour surplus, alongside massive variations in demand for labour at the docks, created both uncertainty and irregular working patterns. As Llewellyn Smith noted at the time, there was no choice but to live with that uncertainty: "The docks are residual employments which stand as buffers between ordinary productive industry and the poor house. They are the refuge of the members of other industries who have failed whether from their fault or their misfortune."[18]

It was the young person who carried the burden of this industrial and economic turmoil. In 1901, approximately 20% of London dock labourers who faced the uncertainty of irregular pay and ignominy of harsh and unrelenting work conditions were aged between 15-25.[19] Young women and girls fared no better than young men and boys, locked as they were into an alternating routine of seasonal factory work: jam and confectionary followed by match-making on a rotating basis. The demand for boy labour also increased poverty in London, despite the introduction of the 1870 Education Act, which reduced the pool of juvenile labour, concentrating the supply to the ages of 13 to 19.[20] Analysing returns made in 1899 for a House of Commons Report, it was noted that, at school-leaving age, 40% became shop boys, 8% became office boys and clerks and 18% entered building, metal, wood, clothier and printing trades.[21] A consideration of the East End alone reveals a higher reliance on low-paid, exploitative manual labour amongst the same age group. Self-evidently, alleviation of poverty would have to begin with ministry amongst the young.

Philanthropic Activity in East London

Whilst it is impossible to date the genesis of systematic charitable relief efforts in London with any real certainty, it is notable that the 1860s marked a watershed. This was primarily in compassionate response to the devastating 1866 cholera epidemic – which killed 3,909 Eastenders[22] - but also with moves afoot to legislate for better housing and sanitation. Coupled with the Metropolitan Common Poor Fund, set up the previous year, concern was growing in some quarters for the needs of the poor in the city. Certainly by the beginning of our period, efforts to provide relief were well established. In his excellent book, *East End 1888*, Fishman made an astute comment when he stated that "The one growth industry in East London, at this time of social distress, was charity. Armed with the bible and the bread basket, an army of individual and institution-based philanthropists marched across the City borders to aid...the growing armies of the poor."[23]

As Fishman hinted, Christians were at the forefront of this philanthropic and charitable endeavour. In the Docks, for example, the sheer quantity of Irish Catholics meant that the Church carried an enormous influence: even more than the emerging Socialist and Trade Union movement. As Stedman Jones wryly commented, "Casual workers…remained readier to listen to a few well-chosen homilies from Cardinal Manning than to a torrent of speeches from the S.D.F."[24] Nevertheless, there was a clear divide, even in the mind of charitable Christians, between the deserving poor and the undeserving poor: those who were suffering and unemployed as victims of circumstance and those who were considered to be beyond any reasonable help. This thinking underpinned ensuing social strategies, most especially those advocated by Charles Booth. Two Reports had been published – in

1877 (*Soup Kitchens – the Report of the Sub-committee of the C.O.S.*) and 1879 (*A Soup Kitchen in St. Giles – A Report by the St. Giles Committee on the condition and character of recipients of soup relief*) – both of which suggested that indiscriminate charity was still prevalent in the East End.[25] Activists roundly condemned such activity, as we shall see below, for worsening the situation and increasing pauperism. The Church was at the forefront of that condemnation. Reverend J.R. Green, Vicar of Stepney at the turn of the century noted that, "It is not so much poverty that is increasing in the East, as pauperism, the want of industry, of thrift or self-reliance…Some half a million of people in the East End of London have been flung into the crucible of public benevolence and have come out of it simple paupers."[26]

Nevertheless, philanthropic activity, in a pre-Welfare State age, was crucial. Eagar did not overestimate its importance when he stated that, "Philanthropy provided Education, Pensions, Hospitals, Dispensaries, Soup Kitchens, Free Dinners, Nursing, Thrift Societies, Penny Banks, Lunatic Asylums, Penitentiaries, Reformatories, Asylums and Homes, Home Visiting Agencies, Charities for Clothing and Apprenticeship and Relief in multifarious forms. Even the harshest utilitarians approved the principle of philanthropy, and Christians generally saw its scope and vigour sure evidence of the truth of evangelical religion."[27]

Every Boy's Club and Institute, every Settlement, sought financial support from Victorian gentlemen, peers of the realm and royalty. Without that support, the works would have failed. The thought of failure disquieted those involved in such ministry. Not only would the Gospel message go unheeded but also this spiritual vacuum would be filled by political radicalism, harmful to society but also the well-being of the 'ignorant poor' who knew no better. The Archbishop of York was speaking for a wider Christian constituency when, in 1878, he unashamedly declared, “If we in the Church of England do not deal with the masses, the masses will deal with us.”[28] Such a comment may appear somewhat arrogant when viewed from a twenty-first-century perspective. However, in an age of civil strife, political radicalism and the constant threat of war, the desire for national stability was a natural bed-partner for evangelical religion. If philanthropic activity, most especially amongst the young, could provide both national security and Christian maturity, then it was a worthwhile work indeed.

Conclusion

The ensuing chapters of this book will examine in greater depth the influence of philanthropic activism in East London, most especially as it was directed towards ministry amongst the young. We conclude this part by giving only the briefest consideration to three particular issues, namely: the motivation, spirituality and effect of such activity amongst the needy.

First, in considering exactly what it was that motivated philanthropic activity, we note the revisionist trend amongst many historians to stress the more negative aspects of their endeavours. It is sometimes claimed for these pioneers, as with those missionaries who took the Gospel overseas, that they were little more than ‘gentlemen at play’, bringing with them somewhat condescending and patronising attitudes in an attempt to raise the morality of the poor to a more civilised standard: a religious and cultural imperialism of sorts. It is hoped that the examples given throughout this book will show the gross inaccuracy of this view. Certainly, there were some who were motivated in part by fear of what the *status quo* might bring unless the effects of poverty were eliminated. We have already made reference to the Archbishop of York. Samuel Smith, a philanthropist supporting charitable endeavours in the East End, revealed similar anxieties in 1885: "I am deeply convinced that the time is approaching when this seething mass of human misery will shake the social fabric, unless we grapple more earnestly with it that we have yet done...The proletariat may strangle us unless we teach it the same virtues which have elevated the other classes of society."[29] Whilst many others would concur with that view, few suggested that this was the *primary* motivation for philanthropic activity. The motivation for most activists was profoundly informed by their spirituality, which differed according to churchmanship.

For those of an Evangelical persuasion, the focus was primarily soteriological. As Worrall succinctly summarised, "they believed that individual salvation would be the beginning of social reform, and that as individuals adopted the life which God intended for them their material circumstances would improve."[30] Such was the motivation for William Smith, a Sunday School teacher in Glasgow who, after taking a particularly rowdy class in 1883, had decided upon starting the Boys Brigade. Such had been the motivation for Josiah Spiers who set up the Children's Special Service Mission after having seen the ministry of American evangelist Payson Hammond in 1867.[31] One hardly need detail the already well-documented examples of such Evangelical social reformers as Shaftesbury and Barnardo to elucidate the point. The Congregationalist minister Andrew Mearns expressed the concern of the Evangelical constituency in *Bitter Cry of Outcast London*: "The churches are making the discovery that seething in the very centre of our great cities, concealed by the thinnest crust of civilisation and decency, is a vast mass of moral corruption, of heartbreaking misery and absolute godlessness, and that scarcely anything has been done to take into this awful slough the only influences that can purify or remove it."[32] The task of the Evangelical was to reverse that trend by leading the poor into a relationship with the Living God.

The huge swathe of Anglo-Catholic priests ministering in slum districts found motivation from a different emphasis. Again, it is Worrall who summarised their position so well: "The theology of the movement stressed the incarnation of Christ as God's amazing condescension to mankind. It was a natural corollary that his representatives should also be seen to throw in their lot with the poorest and meanest elements in society."[33] So it was that the Anglo-Catholic philanthropists and priests dedicated themselves to the imitation of Christ: providing physical as well as spiritual relief; meeting the material needs of the people primarily through the provision of soup kitchens, medical aid and schooling.

Regardless of churchmanship, the overall effectiveness of philanthropic activity in East London has always been a moot point. To be sure, much immediate distress was relieved through these endeavours. Financial support in the East End was of great importance in 1860, when a severe winter led to a cessation of all river work and private relief was controlled through the police courts.[34] In 1866, there was a Mansion House Relief Fund set up to distribute £15,000 in the district.[35] Many similar examples could be cited from that time until the outbreak of the First World War. However, there was considerable concern as to the long-term effects of indiscriminate charity. Few critics would have gone so far as Brooke Lambert from St. Mark's, Whitechapel, who preached an extraordinary sermon at Oxford on the dangers of such philanthropic behaviour: "Some of us East End clergy dread the coming winter like the return of some intermittent fever. The amount of charity which has flowed from West to East, has demoralized the clergy and pauperised the yet honest poor...*The marvel of Christ's life is his repression of his powers of benevolence*."[36] Nevertheless, it was widely recognised that the creation of a culture of dependency was not a viable vision for the future. Dr Guy offered one example of that concern: "If...you will somehow contrive to handcuff the indiscriminate alms-giver, I will promise you for reason I could assign, these inevitable consequences, no destitution, lessened poor rates, prisons emptier, fewer gin shops, less crowded mad houses, sure signs of underpopulation, and an England worth living in."[37] Samuel Barnett, of whom much more will be written in the next chapter, offered the most considered and spiritually envisioned perspective: "If, instead of official giving we can substitute the charity of individuals given in adequate amounts, and to those who are proven to be in need, but given by individuals to individuals, those who give and those who receive will be better for the meeting: human sympathy will add power to the gift, and break down the barrier which makes each class say, 'I am, and none else beside me.'"[38] It was that vision of empowerment, empathy and the breaking down of social and spiritual barriers that underpinned East London youth ministry over the following seventy-five years. It is to the consideration of this trend that we now tu

---

NOTES

[1] A great deal of literature is available. The following, some of which were cited in the *Introduction*, are only a representative sample: W.J. Fishman, *East End 1888*, (London: Duckworth, 1988); Hanks, *God's Special Army: The Story of William Booth*; Hattersley, *Blood and Fire: The Story of William and Catherine Booth and their Salvation Army*; E.G. Howarth & M. Wilson (compilers), *West Ham - A Study in Social and Industrial Problems*, (London: J.M. Dent, 1907); O'Neill, *My East*

End; Powell, *The Man Who Didn't Go to China*; Wagner, *Barnardo*, and Williams, *Barnardo of Stepney*

[2] Stedman Jones, *Outcast London*, p.159

[3] Dock development will be detailed in Chapter 3. For a comprehensive analysis of the impact of Victorian rail development on London, see J.R. Kellett, *The Impact of Railways on Victorian Cities*, (London: Routledge & Kegan Paul, 1969)

[4] Stedman Jones, *Outcast London*, p.325

[5] A statistic cited by Booth in *Life and Labour of the People of London*, (1902), 1st series, vol. 3, p.102

[6] Stedman Jones, *Outcast London*, p.148

[7] An abridged version of the findings has been published in *Charles Booth On the City: Physical Pattern and Social Structure*, (Chicago: Phoenix, 1967), edited by Harold W. Pfautz

[8] G.B. Longstaff, 'Rural Depopulation', *Journal of the Royal Statistical Society*, vol. lvi, September 1893

[9] For a comprehensive analysis, see M.J. Daunton, *House and Home in the Victorian City*, (London: Edward Arnold, 1983)

[10] Stedman Jones, *Outcast London*, p.219

[11] H.J. Dyos, cited by Daunton, *House and Home in the Victorian City*, p.288

[12] Stedman Jones, *Outcast London*, p.330

[13] Stedman Jones, *Outcast London*, p.285

[14] Stedman Jones, *Outcast London*, p.15f.

[15] Stedman Jones, *Outcast London*, p.320

[16] Stedman Jones, *Outcast London*, p.93

[17] S. Gerali in *Agenda for Youth Ministry*, edited by D. Borgman and C. Cook, (London: SPCK, 1998), p.36

[18] Cited by Booth in *Life and Labour of the People of London*, 1st series, vol. 3, p.88

[19] I have based this figure on statistics presented by Stedman Jones in *Outcast London*, p.68

[20] Stedman Jones, *Outcast London*, p.72

[21] Royal Commission, *Poor Laws*, Appendix, vol. xx, Cyril Jackson, 'Report on Boy Labour' (1909), p.4

[22] Stedman Jones, *Outcast London*, p.102

[23] W.J. Fishman, *East End 1888*, p.230

[24] Stedman Jones, *Outcast London*, p.348

[25] Stedman Jones, *Outcast London*, p.273

[26] J.R. Green, *Stray Studies*, Second Series (1904), pp.127, 137

[27] Eagar, *Making Men*, p.25

[28] Cited by Davies, *From Voluntaryism to Welfare State*, (Leicester: National Youth Agency, 1999), p.10

[29] S. Smith, 'The industrial training of destitute children' *Contemporary Review* vol. xlvii, January 1885

[30] B.G. Worrall, *The Making of the Modern Church*, (London: SPCK, 1988), p.41

[31] Spiers' story is related by N. Sylvester in *God's Word in a Young World*, (London: Scripture Union, 1984), p.12

[32] A. Mearns, *Bitter Cry of Outcast London*, October 1883, p.1

[33] Worrall, *The Making of the Modern Church*, p.42

[34] Stedman Jones, *Outcast London*, p.245

[35] Stedman Jones, *Outcast London*, p.246

[36] Brooke Lambert, *East London Pauperism, a Sermon to the University of Oxford*, 1868 (italics mine)

[37] Cited by Stedman Jones, *Outcast London*, p.245

---

[38] S. Barnett, 'Outdoor Relief', *Poor Law Conferences* (1875), p.58

Chapter Two

Youth Ministry in East London

We have thus far noted the inevitable response of those motivated by a Christian conscience to seek the alleviation of the problems and the tending of the needs of those who were suffering social deprivation in the East End of London. In this chapter, we will turn from a general survey of such activism towards a focus on the development of youth ministry. Having already provided the *context*, our task is now to outline the *trend* of such work amongst young people. First, we shall consider the impact of the Settlement Movement. Second, we will detail the formation of Boys' Clubs. Third, we shall examine the type of youth ministry offered by local parish churches in East London during our period. Fourth, we shall explore the creative ministry offered through public school missions before drawing our conclusions.

The Settlement Movement

The Settlement Movement was a predominant feature of city life towards the end of the nineteenth-century and into the mid-twentieth century. By 1926, there were at least fifty-six Settlements in Britain with forty-one in London alone. These Settlements resulted almost exclusively from the efforts of a privileged people who sought to "do a little to remove the inequalities of life."[1] Men and women with the privileges of education wanted to live amongst the poor, learn with them, develop friendships and do what they could to alleviate the suffering that arose through social deprivation. Settlements usually took the form of a large building in a poor city area. From that base, charitable, recreational and educational work was undertaken in the local community. In addition, undergraduates and new graduates were encouraged to stay in the Settlement hostel to assist the work and gain first hand experience of slum conditions and the needs of the socially deprived. An early definition was that, "A settlement is simply a means by which men or women may share themselves with their neighbours; a club-house in an industrial district, where the condition of membership is the performance of a citizen's duty; a house among the poor, where residents may make friends with the poor."[2]

The first such Settlement was established by Samuel Barnett in Whitechapel, East London, in 1884. Barnett, whose wisdom was cited at the end of the previous chapter, was from a wealthy family. His father was a manufacturer of iron bedsteads and his mother came from a Bristol merchant family. He was educated at Wadham College, Oxford, studying law and modern history. After travelling in America, Barnett was ordained in 1867 and served as Curate at St. Mary's, Bryanston Square in London. He was immediately confronted by the social problems of urban life and, in 1869, founded the Charity

Organization Society, through the work of which he met his future wife, Henrietta, who wholeheartedly shared in his ministry. Upon moving to St. Jude's, Whitechapel, Barnett became aware of the huge chasm between religious tradition and the daily experience of the poor. His attempts to reach the socially deprived people of the area were considered unorthodox but he was well supported by his Bishop, Dr. Walsham How. Barnett introduced art exhibitions to Whitechapel, built a parish library and developed schooling in the area. His concern was also for the living conditions of the parishioners. Barnett promoted the *Artisans Dwellings Act 1875* and administrated poor relief in Whitechapel. In 1883, he advocated a universal pension and sought ways to reduce unemployment. Crucially, Barnett also established a Children's Country Holiday Fund, which had an enormous impact on the young people within his parish.

It was out of these efforts that Toynbee Hall was founded in 1884, the model upon which all future Settlements were either built or measured against. According to Pimlott,[3] Toynbee Hall was set up to further three specific aims: scientific research concerning poverty, the furthering of wider lives through education and an enhancement of leadership in the local community. In this sense, Toynbee Hall was ultimately very successful, spawning such future leaders as William Beveridge, R.H. Tawney and Clement Atlee. Barnett's vision had been to create an East London 'working man's university', with great emphasis placed on educational and vocational classes, debates and discussions in its early days. By the mid 1890s, however, attendances began to decline and this aspect of the work had ceased entirely by 1913. Nevertheless, Barnett and those involved with Toynbee Hall never lost the belief that local government structures could be affected for the good by educating the local community and the impact of the Toynbee Hall work was vast indeed.

Not all Settlements followed the Toynbee Hall pattern. Oxford House focussed on working with boys and men. The Passmore Edwards Settlement set up play centres in London and established a school for children with physical disabilities. The Bermondsey Settlement founded the Guild of Play to teach children under the age of ten folk songs and dances.[4] Women's Settlements eventually outnumbered those for men and boys. The Women's University Settlement (now Blackfriars) began in 1887 with the objective of promoting welfare and giving women and children "additional opportunities for education and recreation".[5] Some Settlements were for both sexes. Kingsley Hall, established in 1915 by Muriel and Doris Lester, is one such example. This developed in much the same style as an ashram, not least because of Muriel Lester's experience as a guest of Mohandas K. Gandhi at Ahmedabad. (Gandhi later returned the gesture of friendship by staying at Kingsley Hall for three months in 1931 during a period of negotiation with the British Government). Barnett, in assessing the impact of Settlements in 1898,[6] suggested three primary reasons for their success.

First, that, "Many people become distrustful of the machinery for doing good...They heard the "bitter cry" of the poor; they were conscious something wrong [sic] underneath modern progress; they realised that free trade, reform bills, philanthropic activity, and missions had made neither health nor wealth. They were drawn to do something for the poor."[7] Specifically, University men had recognised the deficiency of charitable work in the name of evangelistic religion. Indiscriminate philanthropy, already recognised as pauperising the receiver, was deemed by Barnett to spiritually pauperise the giver too:

"Drop in a coin, and the duty to a neighbour was done. But duty so done proved often more harmful than helpful...The best-devised mechanism can have neither eyes nor feeling. It must act blindly, and cannot evoke gratitude."[8] Benevolence was often patronising and existing missions sometimes assumed superiority over those amongst whom they lived and worked. Others, however, were moved to fellowship with the poor and did not want to appear as benefactors or missionaries in that same way. Those with a tender social conscience wanted to find new ways of fulfilling their social responsibilities and Settlements seemed to be a way of realising that aspiration.

Second, there "was a demand for more accurate information as to the condition of the people, as to their thoughts and their hopes."[9] There was much talk of social deprivation and the needs of the poor but those who were minded to make an impact on the situation were not content with secondary descriptions. The rise in scientific endeavour demanded a scientific approach to the issue: one in which data could be gathered and real needs met with real solutions. As Barnett, stressed, "it required facts and figures - critical investigation into the causes of poverty and personal knowledge of the poor."[10] Those concerned could only achieve that by actually living in the areas of deprivation themselves and sharing first-hand experience of the problems.

Third, Barnett pointed to the strength of the human spirit and its innate desire to reach beyond boundaries in helping fellow humans. With typical nineteenth-century fervour, he commented that "Nowhere is the growth of this human spirit more evident than at the Universities."[11] Settlements were a genuine attempt to devise a method by which one human spirit could meet another across the divide of class, wealth and social position. In conclusion, Barnett stated that, "A settlement, by bringing into a neighbourhood people whose training makes them sensible to abuses, and whose humanity makes them conscious of other needs, does what machinery as machinery cannot do. It fits supply and demand; it adapts itself to changing circumstances; it yields and goes forward; it follows or guides, according to the moment's need; it turns an organisation which might be a mere machine into a living human force. Above all, it brings men into touch with men, and, by making them fuller characters, enriches their work."[12]

The Formation of Boys' Clubs

Clubs were a standard feature of the East End in the transitional period between nineteenth- and twentieth century. By 1888, there were twenty-three clubs in Whitechapel alone; proprietorial, political and philanthropic.[13] Given the latter type, it is perhaps not surprising that muscular Christianity abounded but it would be an anachronistic caricature to portray that as the whole picture. There was an abundance of purely social clubs, many activities catering for women and young girls as well as a Jewish Working Men's Club, catering for 1,400 immigrants in Great Alie Street, Aldgate.[14]

The history of the national growth and development of Boys' Clubs has been comprehensively outlined in Eagar's excellent book *Making Men*,[15] and it is not our purpose to duplicate that work here. Nevertheless, our later consideration of youth ministry at Dockland Settlement No. 1 must be seen as part of a trend of rapidly mushrooming youth club ministry across London as a whole and East London in particular. The growth in this work was due not least to the creative influence of Tom Pelham, an Old Etonian who, upon his arrival in London in 1870, dedicated himself to the School and Home in Castle Street run by Quentin Hogg. Recognising that "The State does nothing for them, the Church has hitherto done but little, and the chief endeavours to help the young have been due to private endeavour,"[16] the London Diocesan Council and the Diocesan Welfare Council, founded in 1884, sought to support the Clubs and Institutes and three hundred parochial institutions for young people within the Diocese of London. Pelham was instrumental in encouraging this work and created frames of reference and modes of operation for those running clubs. His preference, opposed to the Manchester experience, was for "small, local Institutes, which should never be allowed to outgrow the personal influence of the workers."[17] His was a relational model of youth ministry, in which "Personal influence is one of the first conditions of success."[18] To that end, most of the London Boys' Clubs were managed by committee but run by one committed individual.

Support for this demanding and sacrificial ministry also came from The London Federation of Working-boys' Clubs and Institutes. This body had its first Executive Committee meeting in April 1888, under the guiding hand of its President, Hon. Alfred Lyttelton. It was "confessedly at the start an Old School Tie organisation - with a liberal sprinkling of dog-collars,"[19] but for the next fifty years or so, made a phenomenal impact on the work amongst young boys and men. The Federation had three objectives: to provide a forum and network for the interchange of ideas amongst club leaders; to organise competitions between clubs; and to promote religion in the clubs through lectures and classes. Twenty-eight Clubs and Institutes joined at its inauguration, with membership rising to forty-seven by 1890. All the Clubs and Institutes were Anglican, a mixture of evangelical and Anglo-Catholic. Eagar lists all those Clubs and Institutes affiliated to the Federation in 1889 in his book, *Making Men*.[20] For our purposes, it is worth mentioning just those that were situated within a few miles of the Canning Town work, namely: St. Saviour's, Poplar; All Hallows, East India Docks; St. Augustine's, Haggerston; St. John's, Bethnal Green; Webbe Institute, Bethnal Green; Eton Mission; Harrow Mission; Christ Church (Oxford) Mission; Rugby Mission. How many other similar but non-affiliated works were operative at this time is not known. However, extant parochial records suggest an extensive East End movement of Boys' Clubs and Institutes, of which the Canning Town work would become but one more example.

To gain a better understanding of the Boys' Club ministry at this time, it is worth quoting at some length from the First Federation Report, published in 1890: "No branch of charitable work is more productive of good results than the Boys' Clubs. They can, if efficiently managed, be in some degree to the poor what the Public Schools and Universities have been to the rich. They develop, as no other agency can, that *esprit de corps* in which the poor are, for the most part, so lamentably deficient. They afford unequalled opportunities for those who have received a good education to bring their influence to bear on their poorer brethren at an age when they are most in want of training and direction; they enable hundreds of boys to steer clear of many of the temptations by which the poor of our large towns are constantly surrounded; they offer wholesome recreation to those who otherwise would have few pleasures, or only such pleasures as are vicious and degrading. Indeed, it is not too much to say that on the Elementary Schools, the Polytechnics and the Boys' Clubs the future of the working-classes in England largely depends."[21]

Concerning the day-to-day running of clubs, primary emphasis was placed on competitive activities, most especially sports. Cricket was the most popular, since football was not to become a universal game for some years yet. Swimming, boxing and gymnastics were actively encouraged and, reflecting the foundational public school ethos, club-runs and rowing were not unusual. Almost every club had the inevitable 'drum and fife band', which took its place alongside other entertainments such as brass bands, minstrel troupes, amateur dramatics, draughts, chess and bagatelle. All Clubs conscientiously promoted religion and some - not least the Eton Mission Club - placed considerable emphasis on educational activities, holding classes in geography, history, physical science and natural history.[22]

The impact of these Clubs and Institutes in the East End, and indeed throughout Britain, was simply immense. Lives and communities underwent a radical transformation through the sacrificial ministry of those who were willing and able to devote themselves to the underprivileged in that way. It is beyond the scope of this present work to detail that impact any further. However, it would be pleasant to end with an anecdote that goes some way towards proving the longevity of such ministry. In the biography that she wrote of her husband, Mrs. Henrietta Barnett of Whitechapel commented that, "Up to the end of his life some of the St. Mary's boys remained my husbands friends, bringing their children to see us, and rarely missing the Abbey services when he preached. Sometimes gifts would arrive with notes such as the following: *December* 31 1884. - From three of your "old boys," who often think of you and pray God bless you. C.W. Honeychurch, George S. Hunt, J. Phillips."[23] It is the lives of such as these three anonymous East End lads that bear witness to the philanthropic dedication of Club and Institute workers at the turn of the nineteenth-century and beyond.

Parochial Ministry

Notwithstanding the valuable work of Settlements, Clubs and Institutes, the local parish church continued to be the most direct way by which Christian charity and spiritual ministry could be administered to young people in need. Given the upsurge in employment possibilities and population, it is not surprising that the mid- to late-nineteenth century was a time of great transition for the Church of England in the East End of London. Until 1844, West Ham, the geographical area with which we are primarily concerned in this book, had been a single parish within the diocese of London. Two years later, Essex - except the Barking Deanery - was transferred to the diocese of Rochester where it remained until 1877, when it was again transferred, this time to the newly formed diocese of St. Albans. Spiritual responsibility for the area was given to the Bishop of Colchester until 1901, when the suffragan Bishopric of Barking was formed, with the title vested in the ministry of Bishop Thomas Stevens.[24] Following a 1908 Act of Parliament, the Diocese of Chelmsford was created in February 1914 and the Barking Suffragan Episcopal Area was transferred within its boundaries, where it has remained until today.[25]

We shall be giving detailed consideration to the youth ministry of St. Luke's, Victoria Dock, Canning Town in the next chapter. We would do well at this point, however, to note the broad range of youth activities undertaken in East London parish churches during our period. Given the limited nature of our enquiry, it will suffice to survey the activities of just one 'typical' East End church: St. Paul's, Stratford New Town. A backstreet church built in response to the burgeoning railworker population of the late nineteenth-century, St. Paul's most perfectly represents an average church in our period: lacking any prestige in terms of notable clergy or, indeed, any patronage from philanthropists or nobility. The youth ministry undertaken at St. Paul's would have been considered unremarkable at the time but the briefest of considerations will show just how dedicated local churches of this ilk were to providing for the young.

In his 1901 *Vicar's Letter* to the parish, Reverend W.H. Hewett concluded his review of the previous twelve month's activities by stating that, "A reference to the brief accounts prefixed to the various branches of Parochial Organization… goes to show that in most departments real and satisfactory progress has been made."[26] That was not least the case with the work amongst young people. The Boys Sunday Schools – with 20 teachers – had 250 on their books whilst the Girls Sunday Schools – enjoying the attention of 6 extra teachers – boasted a membership of 315. The Mission Hall Sunday Schools had a further 360 members. The St. Paul's Day Schools had 449 Boys and 260 Girls, with a further 380 infants. A range of other youth ministries, designed to enrich both body and soul, supplemented these educational endeavours. The choir had 24 Boy members. The five Bible Classes for Young Men and Women and Senior Scholars (Boys) were habitually well attended; a commendable area of ministry since "It is scarcely possible to attach too much importance to this branch of our work from which we hope and believe fruit is being found, and will yet be found after many days."[27] News from the Girls' Factory Mission was similarly encouraging as "The number of girls attending during the past year was in excess of the year before, and the general behaviour was much better, whilst the attendance at the Bible Class had distinctly increased."[28] The Senior Boys' Band of Hope had 21 names on the register, whilst the Girls' Temperance Society had 32 members. Informing young people about the evils of alcohol was clearly a priority, with a further 250 junior Band of Hope members. The Sowers' Band, with a membership of 51, instructed young people about the work of the Church Missionary Society and encouraged early participation in mission responsibility by asking for a halfpenny per week from each young person. Under the motto "Quit ye like men, be strong" (1 Corinthians 16:13), muscular Christianity was at the heart of sporting provision at St. Paul's. Medals were awarded for athletics, gymnastics, football, cricket and cycling. Non-competitive recreation, with closing Scripture reading and prayer, was enjoyed on a Thursday evening by no fewer than 33 boys. The Girls' Working Party, which only had a membership of 7, seemingly busied themselves with creative arts and playing the piano.[29]

Fifteen years on, the youth population of the East End was becoming decimated as a result of the First World War. It is difficult to gain an accurate picture of the state of St. Paul's youth ministry at that time; the *Vicar's Letter* produced by Reverend William Ferguson explained that, "For economy's sake only the briefest statement is given, and several details which usually appear have been omitted."[30] Nevertheless, the ensuing *Financial Report* gave details of continuing youth ministry through Sunday schools, day schools, Girls' CMS Club, Lads' Club, Cycling Club, Gymnasium, Soup Kitchen and Choir.[31] By 1928, the War was over but the East End had irrevocably altered. Nevertheless, under the leadership of Reverend Cecil Shaw, the commitment to youth ministry at St. Paul's had remained strong. There was still a powerful educational base through the day schools and Sunday schools. Scripture teaching was still given at regular Bible classes. However, the real focus had now shifted towards the uniformed organisations such as Cubs, Scouts, Brownies, Guides, Rangers, Boys' Brigade and Life Boys Company.[32]

To be sure, St. Paul's, Stratford New Town offers just one example of youth ministry offered from a parochial base in East London during our period. But, given the 'unremarkable' nature of the church it remains a prime example of the broad trend of the time and, for our purposes, is well worth the study. The impression we are left with is of a radical and creative commitment to youth ministry offered through local churches, with a keenly developed awareness of the need to undertake a holistic approach, catering for body, mind and soul.

Public School Missions

The growth of public schools, maintained by private endowments, was a development of the latter half of the nineteenth-century. In the 1860s, the *Clarendon Commission* recognised the existence of nine 'Public Schools'. Seven of these were elite boarding institutions, namely: Eton, Harrow, Westminster, Rugby, Winchester, Charterhouse, and Shrewsbury. Two others, St. Paul's and Merchant Taylor's, were London day schools. Thereafter, the existence of public schools and colleges multiplied at a rapid rate. Everett has suggested that, with regard to public schools, "The whole educational process was designed to mould the student into a young Christian Gentleman. Students from these elite institutions provided Oxford and Cambridge with nearly all of their own students, and graduates of those Universities, as a matter of course, dominated the British political and administrative elite."[33] Perhaps it is not surprising, then, that public schools should be at the forefront of social activism and Christian youth work in deprived areas.

Bishop William Walsham How has already been mentioned with regard to his support of Reverend Samuel Barnett's sterling work in Whitechapel. However, no treatment of this period would be complete with such a cursory reference. This remarkable saint is perhaps the only man from this period who may truly be called 'The Father of the East End'. Samuel Barnett described him as "the most popular man in East London, the one man in the crowd of rival philanthropists and politicians whom everyone thoroughly trusted."[34] Walsham How, the son of a solicitor, was educated at Wadham College in Oxford, prior to his ordination in 1846. Thereafter, he served as Curate at Kidderminster and Shrewsbury before becoming Rector at Whittington, Shropshire. He became suffragan Bishop in London in 1879 and remained in that post until his translation to Wakefield a decade later. Apart from his gift for hymnody, Walsham How is best remembered for his sacrificial devotion to the people of East London and his deep concern for children's work and ministry amongst the young, earning him the nickname, "The Children's Bishop". His greatest desire was to seek out the most able clergy and persuade them to serve within the district. He was also concerned to raise awareness of East London in the hearts and minds of Public Schools and Colleges, persuading them to set up Missions in the East End. Were it not for his pioneering dedication and lively faith, the history of the East End, and the lives of the young people living within the districts, would have been very different.

The first such Mission, formed directly out of the persuasive efforts of Walsham How, was the Eton Mission of Hackney Wick in 1880. The first Missioner was Reverend William Carter, who took on a small house and undertaker's shop in Mallard Street. This place became the centre of all activities for the Mallard Street Club[35] and, as such, provided a model for future Public School and College Missions. East End works that followed in the 1880s were the Christ Church Mission at Poplar, the Oxford House in Bethnal Green, Trinity College, Oxford in Stratford and the short-lived Winchester School Mission at London Docks.[36] Some of these were attached to a local parish church but those that acted independently seemed to be far more successful. Indeed, that success was to last throughout our period. Eton Mission operated into the 1960s. Canning Town links with Malvern College (the subject of Chapter Three) carried on until the same decade. Shrewsbury House Mission, which was founded in Bethnal Green in 1896 but relocated to Liverpool seven years later, is still in existence. Others evolved under different names but the work continued with great success.

Conclusion

Given the social status of those who involved themselves in urban youth ministry during our period, it is perhaps not surprising that so much anonymity has surrounded their endeavours. They had a natural distaste of self-publicity. Nevertheless, their efforts were intense and, above all, very creative. Young people were the subject of holistic ministry; catering for mind, body and spirit. To a large extent, class prejudices were eradicated and the youngsters in their charge were the recipients of a broad education base. Most important of all, however, was the fact that the Christian faith was taught and modelled in an atmosphere of fun. The youth leaders had to be strong characters to survive the excesses of their environment. The young people of the East End were equally strong-minded. The fusion of energy that was created within those relationships was powerful indeed. This was not least the case in Canning Town and it is to that particular district of East London that we now turn.

NOTES

[1] S.A. Barnett, 'Settlements of university men in great towns. A paper read at St John's, Oxford on 17th November 1883', Oxford: The Chronicle Company. Reprinted in J. Pimlott, *Toynbee Hall. Fifty years*

of social progress 1884 - 1934, (London: J. M. Dent, 1935, pp.266-273), p.272

[2] S.A. Barnett, 'University settlements' in W. Reason (ed.) *University and Social Settlements*, (London: Methuen, 1898), p.11

[3] Pimlott, *Toynbee Hall. Fifty years of social progress 1884 - 1934*, p.11

[4] M. Vicinus, *Independent Women. Work and community for single women 1850 - 1920* (London: Virago, 1985), p.235

[5] Barrett, G., *Blackfriars Settlement. A short history 1887 - 1987*, (London: Blackfriars Settlement, 1985), p.2

[6] Barnett, in W. Reason ed., *University and Social Settlements*, p.11f.

[7] Barnett, in W. Reason ed., *University and Social Settlements*, p.12.

[8] Barnett, in W. Reason ed., *University and Social Settlements*, p.13.

[9] Barnett, in W. Reason ed., *University and Social Settlements*, p.13

[10] Barnett, in W. Reason ed., *University and Social Settlements*, p.13

[11] Barnett, in W. Reason ed., *University and Social Settlements*, p.14

[12] Barnett, in W. Reason ed., *University and Social Settlements*, p.25

[13] Fishman, *East End 1888*, p.306

[14] For details of the extent of this work, see Fishman, *East End 1888*, p.306-311

[15] W. McG. Eagar, *Making Men*, p.238ff.

[16] Dean Farrar, Preface to T. Pelham, *Handbook to Youths' Institutes and Working Boys' Clubs*, (London, 1889)

[17] Cited by Eagar in *Making Men*, p.240

[18] Cited by Eagar, *Making Men*, p.241

[19] Eagar, *Making Men*, p.238

[20] Eagar, *Making Men*, p.265

[21] 1890 Report of the London Federation of Working-boys' Clubs and Institutes, cited by Eagar, *Making Men*, p.253

[22] Eagar, *Making Men*, 258f.

[23] H. Barnett, *Canon Barnett*, Vol. 1, (London: John Murray, 1918), p.26

[24] The life of Thomas Stevens was chronicled by S. G. Wilson in *The First Bishop of Barking*, (Colchester: Benham & Co., 1921)

[25] For details of the creation of the Chelmsford Diocese, see J.T Inskip, *A Man's Job*, (London: Skeffington, 1948). Inskip was the second Bishop of Barking.

[26] W.H. Hewett, *The Record of Another Year's Work ending Dec. 31, 1900, with Illustrations and Statements*, p.6

[27] Hewett, *The Record of Another Year's Work ending Dec. 31, 1900, with Illustrations and Statements*, p.30

[28] Hewett, *The Record of Another Year's Work ending Dec. 31, 1900, with Illustrations and Statements*, p.62

[29] All information in this paragraph was gleaned from Hewett, *The Record of Another Year's Work ending Dec. 31, 1900, with Illustrations and Statements*, pp.1-68

[30] W. Ferguson, *Financial Report for 1915*, p.2

[31] Ferguson, *Financial Report for 1915*, pp.3-15

[32] C.A. Shaw, *Blotter, Calendar and Year Book 1928*

[33] G. Everett, 'Public Schools', www.landow.stg.brown.edu/victorian

[34] Cited by Eagar, *Making Men*, p.81

[35] Eagar, *Making Men*, p.206

[36] For details of all these Missions, see Eagar, *Making Men*, p.206-224

Chapter Three

Youth Ministry in Canning Town

Having provided the context of social activism and philanthropic endeavour in East London and outlined the trend of that activism as it related to youth ministry, we are now in a position to examine a more specific case study of that trend: namely, youth ministry in the East London district of Canning Town. In doing that, we shall consider four primary factors. First, we shall briefly outline the historical development of Canning Town. Second, we shall consider the impact of Settlements on the youth of the area. Third, we will examine the youth activities offered by the local parish church, St. Luke's, Victoria Dock. Finally, we will analyse the youth ministry of Malvern College Mission – the precursor to Dockland Settlement No.1 – before drawing our conclusions.

The Early Development of Canning Town

Canning Town is an East End district that, at the beginning of our period, was located in the heart of the Borough of West Ham. West Ham was an ideal location for many of the anti-social industries that were springing up at the time, as Stedman Jones explained: "Its extensive waterfrontage lessened transport costs; it was within easy distance of London for cartage; it was well provided with railways and docks; and finally…its local authority was deliberately lax in its enforcement of slaughterhouse, building, factory, and smoke regulations."[1]

Canning Town and its two sub-districts - Hallsville and Tidal Basin - was nothing more than marshland until the beginning of these local industrialisation efforts in the 1840s. It was an attractive area upon which to build, both because the marshland was seven feet below high water mark and the Eastern Counties Railway had recently secured the surrounding countryside.[2] From that decade, the rapidity of growth was nothing short of extraordinary. In 1871, the population of the Borough of West Ham was 62,000. Thirty years later that had mushroomed to 267,000 and, by 1925 pre-war figures peaked at 318,500.[3] Much of that growth was focussed on the Dockland areas of Canning Town, Custom House, North Woolwich and Silvertown. An 1857 article in Charles Dickens' *Household Words* entitled, 'Londoners Over the Border', suggested, "Canning Town is the child of the Victoria Docks."[4] Research fifty years later came to a slightly different conclusion, namely that the increase in population "was chiefly due to the Beckton Gas Works and the Thames Iron Works, though the docks probably increased it to some extent."[5] Regardless of which specific industry operated as the primary catalyst, that the community grew as a response to industrial development is undeniable. The Royal Docks (with its sixty-four acres of water),[6] S.W. Silver's factory, the Clyde Wharf sugar refinery, Henry Tate's cube sugar factory, Abraham Lyle's syrup firm, James Keiller's marmalade and confectionery works, the Royal Primrose Soap factory, Brunner Mond's caustic soda plant, Beckton Gas Works and Thames Iron Works. These are just some of the industries that were responsible for development in the Canning Town area in the latter part of the nineteenth-century and upon which the local economy was almost wholly reliant.

Such was the rush of development in this area that planning and control of housing and sanitation was grossly neglected. As early as 1842, the *Chadwick Report* had warned that "the various forms of epidemic, endemic, and other disease caused, or aggravated, [are] propagated chiefly amongst the labouring classes by atmospheric impurities produced by decomposing animal and vegetable substances, by damp and filth, and close and overcrowded dwellings."[7] Nevertheless, terraced housing of the worst possible kind continued to spring up throughout the district with disastrous social consequences.[8] A 1907 study of the Borough of West Ham showed statistically what the inhabitants of Canning Town already knew from bitter experience. Tidal Basin had the most people living per acre than any other part of the Borough. It also had the highest annual death rate at 18.4 per 1000, closely followed by Canning Town at 17.6 per 1000. Canning Town had the second highest infant mortality rate, at 170 per 1000.[9] Tidal Basin, inhabited mainly by casual labourers, was described as "[a] ward [that] consists of small streets running in every direction, with entire lack of design."[10] The detailed description of the area was even more condemning: "The lowest class of loafers and very irregular workers live in the short streets and cul-de-sacs off the Victoria Dock Road...They [live] in a filthy condition with wet walls, and paper peeling off and [have] only sacks for bedding. In some of these houses four families have lived at one time."[11]

A snapshot of the area can be gained by looking at the 1891 Census figures for two Canning Town streets that are of particular importance in the historical development of Dockland Settlement No.1: Cooper Street and Vincent Street. Cooper Street in 1891 had twenty-eight houses, all with less than five rooms. These dwellings accommodated 103 adults and 125 young people aged 20 and under. Vincent Street had forty-four houses, all bar the Tavern with less than five rooms, accommodating 143 adults and 197 young people under the age of 20.[12] Of those 246 adults, only 23 had been born in Canning Town. Crucially, only 11 of those 23 were men,[13] the other 12 being local girls who had married outsiders seeking employment. The other adult inhabitants came to Canning Town mainly from other London districts. Most of England's counties were also represented by inhabitants, as well as one from Australia and another from Canada. Canning Town was a culturally mixed area, with all the joys and tensions that inevitably arose from such circumstances.

Settlements in Canning Town

The Borough of West Ham had the benefit of many Settlements and similar philanthropic institutions by the end of the nineteenth-century.[14] Canning Town was serviced, other than through the Dockland Settlement, primarily by one other Settlement and two recreational facilities. The latter were created by Thames Ironworks[15] and by Henry Tate (in 1887)[16] for their workers in the locality. The Settlement was specifically for Canning Town women and was founded in 1892 by the pastor of the Canning Town Congregational Church, Reverend F.W. Newland.[17] It was closely associated with the Mansfield

House Settlement in the nearby Barking Road and was ably led for thirty years from its inception by Rebecca H. Cheetham. The primary work of the Settlement was to provide health care for women and children.[18]

St. Luke's, Victoria Dock Parish Church

Despite the ever-changing nature of Diocesan boundaries outlined in the previous chapter, there was no lack of good local parochial initiatives in meeting the needs of the increasing population of labourers and their families. In 1857, the Vicar of Plaistow and Sir Antonio Brady had established the Plaistow and Victoria Dock Mission. 1863 saw the creation of the "London over the Border" Fund to provide much needed financial assistance. The following year saw the formation of the parish of St. Mark Silvertown, which included the Victoria Dock/Tidal Basin ward.

Most important of all for our study, however, was the sterling work that would be carried out by St. Luke's, Victoria Dock, under the faithful and effective ministry of Reverend J.C. Buckley, from the 1880s until the end of the First World War. The church founder, Reverend Dr. Henry Boyd had begun work on the church in 1873 to replace an Iron Church built by the Thames Ironworks in 1857. It was consecrated two years later and a separate parish was formed out of St. Mark's. The living was originally vested in the Bishop but, in 1886, transferred to the Lord Chancellor so that All Hallows, London Wall, could support the benefice. St. Matthew's Mission transferred to St. Luke's from St. Mark's and The Ascension Church remained a parish mission until 1905. There was also, from 1887, a Lascar Mission working with Indian sailors coming to the Docks.[19]

By the mid-1880s, St. Luke's had clearly become a vibrant church, integrally involved in shaping the life of the local community. There was a very strong emphasis on youth and children's work. St. Luke's Schools, which had been in existence since the days of the Iron Church, provided exemplary education and were always highly praised by the Annual Schools Inspections.[20] A weekly Children's Service augmented the 11.00 Parish Communion except on the first and third Sundays of the month when the main worship was a Children's Service. There were also Children's services held on Holy Days and Thursday evenings, with more than three hundred young people in regular attendance. These were supplemented with midweek Bible studies for young people, a Girls Perseverance Guild, recreation classes, reading classes, football teams, two swimming clubs, a Drum and Fife Band, an Orchestral Society, a Lawn Tennis Club and the facilities of the Boyd Institute located opposite the main Church building.

In addition to all this local work, the young people of the parish were able to enjoy many days beyond the boundaries of the East End. St. Luke's arranged an annual outing to Epping Forest, usually in July. There were other excursions to places local and not so local: St. Albans, Loughton, Broxbourne, Southend and Waltham Abbey to name but a few.[21] Furthermore, there was a Children's Holiday Fund that enabled many young people to enjoy extended periods away from Canning Town. In July and August 1906, for example, more than sixty children went for a fortnight holiday in the country. Others embarked on pea-picking and fruit and hop gathering.

Malvern College Mission

Set in the context of the Public School Mission movement of the 1880s, we note that the Malvern College Mission in Canning Town was a rather late development in East London and that it followed a well-established trail of pioneer work. Malvern College itself was typical of many public schools founded in the mid- to late-nineteenth century. The Constitution was established in August 1862, the first pupils being admitted in 1865 under the Headship of Reverend Arthur Faber, "a man of strong personality and high intellectual vigour, a shrewd judge of character with the saving grace of humour."[22] Upon Faber's resignation fifteen years later, Reverend C.T. Cruttwell became Headmaster. Since he "was not a successful ruler of men,"[23] numbers at the institution decreased by one-third to only two hundred in the period before his resignation in 1881. Fortunes reversed somewhat under Reverend W. Grundy and, by the arrival of Reverend A. St. J. Gray in 1891, Malvern College was "a school rapidly growing in numbers, and full of life and enthusiasm."[24] An outbreak of diphtheria in the Spring term of 1894, closely followed by an epidemic of influenza one year later, did nothing to quell applications to the school; numbers were at four hundred by 1896. The period 1894-96 saw considerable fabric development at Malvern: first, a cricket pavilion was erected, then a football pitch was purchased.[25] Finally, work begun on building a fine Chapel.

The latter development was perhaps symbolic of the growing sense of religious responsibility at Malvern College, in common with many public schools at the end of the nineteenth-century. The Headmasters at Malvern had all been keenly aware of their duty to nurture boys with a sense of social responsibility; young men who would respond to those in greater need than themselves. To that end, it was decided in 1878 to support the Melanesian Mission but there was little interest in such a geographically distant project. Four years later, efforts were transferred to the parish of All Saints, Haggerston, an area of East London adjacent to Hackney. £80 per annum was contributed towards the cost of a parish nurse but still the school wanted to display a greater level of commitment and involvement. In 1893, Malvern College decided to relocate its efforts to a separate district and found its own Mission. Captain Ben Tinton, who came to the Mission after the First World War, suggested that Canning Town was chosen after a series of newspaper articles tried to find "the worst street in London." The result was that "Vincent Street, Canning Town, a street in a very neglected area in the East End of London, was voted the worst street."[26] A property could not be bought in Vincent Street, so Malvern College purchased a two-room workman's cottage in Cooper Street, which ran parallel.

The Malvern College Mission was established in September 1894. Contrary to Watherston's claim[27] the first full-time Missioner was not Reverend G.F. Gillett but Reverend St. Hill Bourne. Prior to the First World War, he was succeeded by Reverends Gillett, Crookenden, Lee and Tinley.[28] Malvern College initially contributed £200 per year to the work, a sum that had increased to £350 after the War. This was raised through the weekly Chapel offertory and special collections each term and on Speech Day. Personal donations from friends of the School, parents and Old Malvernians took the annual contribution to a staggering £2000 per annum. In return, the Missioner would visit Malvern College each term to report on the work that was being undertaken. In 1898, Gillett described the vision of the Mission as being "...to carry on the church's work amongst her people from both a religious and a social point of view and to be a centre of religious influence and social good."[29]

Given the formidable social work already in place in Canning Town, through the collective ministries of St. Luke's, the Women's

Settlement, and the recreational facilities provided by both Tate and the Ironworks, the Malvern College claim to "have formed a radiant corner of light in a dark and drab neighbourhood"[30] may seem a little self-congratulatory. Nevertheless, the early formation of various Boys' Clubs, a Church Lads' Brigade and Sunday Schools did indeed have an impact on the local community. In addition, the Mission built a small Iron Church and employed a nurse to tend the sick. For the ten years following its foundation, the work of Malvern College Mission struggled on in difficult circumstances, and with various changes in personnel, to the best of its ability. What was clearly needed, however, was a leader of great vision to enhance the work. That leader came in the form of Reginald Kennedy-Cox, whose ministry at Dockland Settlement No.1 will be the subject of our case study.

Conclusion

When assessing the effectiveness of his ministry at the Mayflower Family Centre, David Sheppard has never been keen to claim too much for himself. Sometimes, however, he has been even less keen to claim anything for his predecessors. With laudable, if misguided, frankness he stated in 1967 that, "A vital part of any success God may have given us has been that we have all from the beginning admitted how complete has been the failure of Evangelical Christians in these districts."[31] That comment was surely an unfair appraisal of the creative efforts of Christians throughout the previous seventy-five years in Canning Town. The youth work at Settlements, parish church and Malvern Mission – albeit perhaps not 'Evangelical' in the sense that Sheppard may choose to define the word – was remarkably successful. Young people in the district were nurtured in the faith and had instilled in them Christian values. They were the recipients of good educational endeavours. The abundance of opportunities to escape the East End – even if just for a day or two each year – were seized upon with relish and gratitude. Work amongst youth was a high priority and taken most seriously in Canning Town. Not least was that the case at Dockland Settlement No.1, the specific case study to which we now turn.

NOTES

[1] Stedman Jones, *Outcast London*, p.26

[2] R. Kennedy-Cox, *Through the Dock Gates*, (London: Michael Joseph, 1939), p.18

[3] Statistics taken from D. Sheppard, *Built as a City*, (London: Hodder and Stoughton, 1974) p.101

[4] 'Londoners Over the Border', *Household Words*, No.390, Saturday September 12, 1857, n.p.

[5] E.G. Howarth and M. Wilson (compilers), *West Ham - A Study in Social and Industrial Problems*, (London: J.M. Dent, 1907), p.49

[6] Kennedy-Cox, *Through the Dock Gates*, p.20

[7] *Chadwick Report*, 'From the Poor Law Commissioners on an Inquiry into the Sanitary Conditions of the Labouring Population of Great Britain,' London, 1842, p.369

[8] Contemporary accounts of East End life can be found in the excellent monograph, *One Dinner a Week and Travels in the East*, articles from 'All the Year Round', compiled by Charles Dickens, (London: London Cottage Mission, 1884).

[9] Howarth and Wilson, *West Ham - A Study in Social and Industrial Problems*, p.30

[10] Howarth and Wilson, *West Ham - A Study in Social and Industrial Problems*, p.53

[11] Howarth and Wilson, *West Ham - A Study in Social and Industrial Problems*, p.56

[12] 1891 Census, Public Records Office, Microfiche Reference RG12/1322

[13] The Vincent Street men: No.10, Joseph Hawes (21) - Blacksmith labourer; No.24, Richard Medbury (45) - General labourer; No.50, John Nicholas (33) - Dock labourer; No.52, John Angell (32) - Dock labourer; No.58, Thomas Taylor (25) - Dock labourer; No.86, George Dance (31) - Dock labourer. The Cooper Street men: No.3, John Watson (28) - Dock labourer; No.7, Thomas Simmonds (30) - Carpenter; No.11, Robert Watson (25) - General labourer; No.19, John Middleton (26) - Lighterman; No.26, Albert Sunshine (34) - Stevedore.

[14] For details of philanthropic institutes, settlements and hostels in West Ham, see *West Ham 1886-1986* (The Council of the London Borough of Newham, London: Plaistow Press, 1986), p.141ff.

[15] *Victoria Histories of the Counties of England*, Essex, ii.595

[16] J. Russell, *Hist. Tate Institute, 1887-1933*, (TS 1951)

[17] *The Essex Review*, i.68-9

[18] *The Stratford Express*, 22 March 1913

[19] Details of the work of all these Missions can be found in *St. Luke's Parish, Victoria Docks*, monthly news sheet.

[20] Excerpts from the Annual School Inspectors Reports appear periodically in *St. Luke's Parish, Victoria Docks*, monthly news sheet.

[21] *St. Luke's Parish, Victoria Docks*, news sheets from 1904-1918 contain the details of these trips.

[22] *Malvern College Register 1865-1924*, (ed. H.G.C. Salmon, London: Charles Murray, 1925), p.xi.

[23] *Malvern College Register 1865-1924*, p.xiii

---

[24] *Malvern College Register 1865-1924*, p.xiv

[25] *Malvern College Register 1865-1924*, p.xv

[26] B. Tinton, *War Comes to the Docks*, (London: Marshall, Morgan and Scott, 1941), p.21

[27] P. Watherston, *A Different Kind of Church*, p.17

[28] *Malvern College Register 1865-1924*, p.xxiii

[29] *Old Malvernian*, 1989, n.p.

[30] *Malvern College Register*, p.xxiii

[31] D. Sheppard, *Christians in Industrial Areas - A Correspondence*, No. 1, February 1967, p.4

Chapter Four

Youth Ministry at Dockland Settlement No.1

Thus far, we have focussed almost exclusively on context and trend: exploring the nature of East London during our period, the problems and needs of the young people at that time and the manner in which ministry to the young was carried out through Settlements, Clubs and Institutes, parochial endeavour and Missions. We now come to a considerably more in-depth study of our theme, a case study designed to illuminate in some detail all that we have previously outlined. In examining the youth ministry at Dockland Settlement No.1, we shall move through a number of sections. First, we consider the life and thought of Settlement founder Reginald Kennedy-Cox. Second, we shall examine the youth ministry at the Settlement before the First World War before unfolding similar narratives for the youth ministry between the Wars and after the Second World War. We shall resist the temptation to make conclusions at the end of this chapter since the final chapter will be a more in-depth assessment of the work.

Reginald Kennedy-Cox

Although not the official leader until 1919, Kennedy-Cox's involvement with the Canning Town work began as early as 1904. It is undoubtedly the case that the sheer force and magnetism of his personality was chiefly responsible for the success of the youth ministry in the ensuing thirty years. Kennedy-Cox was a complex person and an understanding of the man must precede an understanding of his work.

Kennedy-Cox was born into a wealthy Somerset family in 1881, the son of a crippled Canadian mother and a devoted husband and father. He was educated at Temple Grove in Richmond before moving to Malvern College. He conceded in his biography that it was his five years at Malvern that was to shape his life[1] although, as we shall see below, that may not have been for the most orthodox of reasons.

After Malvern, Kennedy-Cox went to Hertford College, Oxford, one of the poorest and dependent solely on student fees. Despite that, however, Hertford and its two predecessors - Hart Hall and Magdalen Hall - enjoyed an illustrious alumni. William Tyndale and Alexander Briant represented the martyr traditions of both Protestantism and Catholicism. John Donne and Jonathan Swift represented the arts as Thomas Hobbes did philosophy. Edward Hyde had gone on to serve Charles II as Earl of Clarendon and Henry Pelham had become Prime Minister. Reflection on the successes of these predecessors could not inspire academic prowess in Kennedy-Cox. Even less was he gifted in sporting endeavours. His real abilities were dramatic and his greatest ambition was to become a successful playwright, realising that "the stage provided a wonderful platform from which to influence public opinion."[2]

By his own admission, Kennedy-Cox "passed through [his] Oxford days entirely uninfluenced by the Church."[3] Strangely, given his artistic temperament, he remained unmoved by the High Church party and even more unmoved by his tutor Dean Inge, about whom he punningly commented, "I cannot remember a single wise or witty thing he ever said."[4] Nevertheless, Kennedy-Cox was no atheist. He enjoyed Church, commenting that "The singing at some of the College Chapels was indescribably beautiful."[5] His Christian interest was predominantly humanistic: "I have always been fortunate and very happy. I am grateful for that, and I've wanted to express my gratitude in some tangible way."[6] Interestingly, the Principal of Hertford College during Kennedy-Cox's time was none other than Dr. Henry Boyd, the founder of St. Luke's, Canning Town.[7] It is not unlikely that Kennedy-Cox would have heard details of Boyd's time in the parish and thus a seed may have been sown in his mind from his Oxford experience as well as his time at Malvern College.

Upon moving to the West End of London in 1902, Kennedy-Cox socialised in the most influential theatrical circles. Relishing his new environment, he stated that "I went to practically every first night of the early nineteen hundreds."[8] The first part of his autobiography is a wonderful exercise in 'name-dropping' and those artistes for whom Kennedy-Cox was content "to be always the audience" must have eagerly sought his company![9] He was self-deprecating about his playwright abilities, commenting on his "mild disappointments and perhaps well-deserved humiliations."[10]

Kennedy-Cox was coy about his reasons for leaving the theatre to embark on ministry in Canning Town. "I did not go for any particular reason," he wrote, adding that the radical new lifestyle he embraced was nothing more than "a chance happening."[11] This is surely mere rhetoric, however, since it is hard to believe that such a renunciation of privilege could be an unmotivated act. It seems probable that Kennedy-Cox's understatement was an attempt to divorce himself from those who undertook similar work out of religious zeal and an innate sense of Divine calling. Certainly, Kennedy-Cox claimed no such religious fervour for himself, far less any Damascus Road experience that changed his perspective on life. Rather, he stated only a simplistic belief that "[God] has planned some individualistic piece of work for every creature of His to do. That being the case, I wanted to find my job early in life, whilst I had the vitality and power to do it."[12] In attempting to understand Kennedy-Cox's motivation for involving himself in Canning Town youth ministry, we need to consider three things.

First, he had an innate love of human beings. This is most clearly revealed in the format of his autobiography. Few dates are given to chart the course of his life. Rather, Kennedy-Cox was concerned to provide "a human document" that would be a "narrative...in the form of a film, a silent film, one of the early ones."[13] As such, the recurring details are not so much the events of his life as the wonderful eccentricities of those with whom he had come into contact over the years. Quite simply, Kennedy-Cox relished interacting with interesting people and was energised by such contact. In a telling comment, his lifelong friend, Edward Knoblock, suggested that when Kennedy-Cox first encountered the Dockland community, its inhabitants "made instantaneous appeal to [his] spirit of adventure. They became a challenge to him."[14]

Second, Kennedy-Cox was, like many of his peers, influenced by Platonic idealism. This is not surprising, given the nature of his education and dramatic interests. Knoblock, commenting on his attraction to Canning Town, recognised Kennedy-Cox's understanding that, "What these men and women, these growing boys and girls lacked most of all in their daily lives was "Beauty." They were hungry for it, outwardly and inwardly. Yes, outwardly - inwardly: that was the order. Give these people some place in which to meet where beauty, cleanliness, peace were to be found, then the spirit would soon grow and blossom."[15]

Looking back on his ministry, Kennedy-Cox concluded that he had "fought passionately to smash up the slums and to substitute beauty for the drab ugliness of industrial London."[16] Perhaps his greatest gift was an ability to recognise the beauty within those amongst whom he lived and worked. His lifelong desire was to create a social setting that would reflect their inward beauty and enable it to develop.

Third, it is likely that Kennedy-Cox was, in part, motivated by his love of drama. We gain an insight into Kennedy-Cox's character in his candid admission that "I have always been interested in crime as well as in the theatre. I suppose that it is the drama in both which makes its appeal to me."[17] Perhaps it is not surprising, then, that he should have been profoundly affected by witnessing an incident at the Old Bailey courts in London. Waiting to meet a friend, Kennedy-Cox drifted into one courtroom where a young man was being sentenced to death for a crime of passion. Whilst he claimed that "it was not my dramatic instinct that was aroused," Kennedy-Cox went on to relate the tale with his characteristic eye for detail, suspense and tragedy.[18] Incensed by the lack of compassion exhibited by the barristers in the courtroom, Kennedy-Cox was deeply moved by the plight of the young man. However, it was not a sense of philanthropic duty that pierced his mind so much as an overwhelming sense of self-realisation. As he described it, "I think I saw myself then at the Old Bailey quite clearly for probably the first time in my life...The things that I regarded as worth striving for now seemed amazingly trivial and foolish."[19] Watherston oversimplifies the course of history by referring to this event as "the turning point in bringing him down to Canning Town."[20] Nevertheless, it was a defining moment for Kennedy-Cox and played no small part in resetting the direction of his life.

After this experience at the Old Bailey, Kennedy-Cox joined a friend he called the Marquis in feeding the homeless on the Embankment, under the auspices of the Church Army.[21] Indicative of his drama-loving character, he referred to this activity as "our great adventure."[22] Even more telling is that their first experience of this work took place at 11.15 p.m., after an outing to the theatre! Kennedy-Cox recalled that he "started off, very diffident but intensely interested, and soon terribly saddened by the piteous scene presented by these outcast men."[23]

He began to realise that the drama of life was far more powerful than any he could write for the West End audiences. Later, he was to comment on his desire "to go down to a slum and by living there try to learn something more about life - *real life*, not just the kind of thing I had been writing about."[24] Fitting it was, then, that it should be the meeting of these two worlds that finally led Kennedy-Cox to Canning Town. When one of his stage plays got to London, he was encouraged by the leading lady to do what he could to fill the upper stalls. Kennedy-Cox wrote to the Malvern College Missioner, inviting him to bring his young people to a performance. The evening was such a success that "We became the best of friends in the shortest possible time. I flattered myself that they liked me, and I certainly knew that I liked them."[25] In a subsequent visit to these people in their home environment, Kennedy-Cox became convinced that he should "chuck all this play-writing business - no more first nights, white gardenias and nodding to friends in the stalls."[26] His arrival in East London marked the beginning of a new phase for youth work at the Malvern College Mission in particular and Canning Town in general.

Before moving on to a consideration of the ministry of Kennedy-Cox at the Malvern College Mission and Dockland Settlement, there is one more aspect of his personality that must be considered. It is this that relates most pertinently to his claim that Malvern College shaped his life more than Oxford University, namely: his passionate involvement with occult practices and the Freemasons. Evidence for this is understandably scarce and well-hidden but, nevertheless, compelling.

His first experience of occult practice occurred at Malvern. Wandering through the town on a restless afternoon, he came across a fortune-teller. Intrigued, he entered her room and had the future revealed to him: "She saw me always surrounded by crowds. I was speaking to them, always speaking, tremendously in earnest, and always in the South of England, never north. In the north there would be failure. "Keep away from the north; go to America if you like, you will be fortunate there, but it is the South of England, and the people there, that you must trust. Don't marry, that would mean tremendous unhappiness...There is only one great illness in your life, passed, I think; there is one more to come, but not so serious. You need never fear fire or water, but death will come to you in a strange way, a violent way; it may be murder, it will be swift and violent."[27]

The importance of this experience for Kennedy-Cox cannot be overestimated. First, he recognised the illness as being his boyhood bout of enteric fever.[28] Second, it was a conscious decision of his not to marry. Third, Kennedy-Cox devoted a great deal of time and energy in later years fund-raising for the Dockland Settlement Movement in America.[29] Fourth, it was the warning of the fortune-teller that governed the policy of his Settlement developments: "I have often been asked to embark upon a venture at Liverpool, but I have always remembered the little old lady's words, "Beware of the north - you will never prosper there.""[30]

At Oxford, his curiosity in the occult was further aroused by Lord Hugh Cecil who came to debate the existence or otherwise of ghosts. Jack Pigott, a contemporary of Kennedy-Cox, claimed that his family home had a ghost and so it was decided that the two of them, with the war-correspondent Ernest Bennett, would try an experiment with the apparition. Spending three days at the house, Kennedy-Cox reported that, during one night, "my Irish terrier, which had seemed to me to have been dozing quietly at my feet, opened his eyes wide and listened intently. There wasn't a sound. He remained motionless but very alert. Slowly his hair began to bristle and I clutched the edge of my chair...The dog leapt quietly off the chair and advanced up the room in the light of the fire, walking towards the very spot where we had been told there was a panel in the wall, and pausing there, stiff and alert. Slowly his bristles subsided."[31] The ghost did not appear but the event clearly had an impact on Kennedy-Cox to warrant so many pages in his autobiography.

Perhaps the most compelling evidence for Kennedy-Cox's involvement in occult practices is found in the *Daily Telegraph* obituary for the witch, Cecil Williamson. His association with witchcraft is well-documented, to the extent that he opened two witchcraft museums, on the Isle of Man and in Windsor. His experimentation is linked primarily to that of fellow occultist Aleister Crowley, who, like Kennedy-Cox, was an Old Malvernian. The obituary states that, "[Williamson] gained a wider experience of the occult world when he was befriended by a philanthropist named Kennedy Cox...At the suggestion of Kennedy Cox, Williamson was recruited to assist, as "The Boy in White", Madame De La Haye, a well-known medium. His job was to provide answers, supposedly as an oracle for messages from the spirit world, "while dressed in a sort of white Eton suit, with my hair floured".[32] Given Williamson's age at the time, this friendship with Kennedy-Cox must have begun in the early-1920s. Years later, Williamson was to become "Witch Protector to the Royal House of Windsor". As such, he ministered witchcraft to the Royal family with various rituals, including the use of a toad. Whilst this work was inherited from the previous "Protector", Rosa Woodman, it is certainly the case that Kennedy-Cox too was well acquainted with the Royal Family. There is no recorded evidence as to whether he practised witchcraft within those aristocratic circles.

Kennedy-Cox suggested an involvement with Freemasonry in his autobiography. He related an incident during his time at Oxford, concerning Cecil Rhodes of South Africa: "When he died he sent back his old Masonic apron to our Oxford Lodge, of which he was a member. I was there when it arrived..."[33] Furthermore, there was established in 1904 a Bishop of Barking Masonic Lodge[34] that met in Canning Town. Given the scarcity of large rooms at the time, it is most likely that Dockland Settlement No.1 was the location of that Lodge. Perhaps it was the Masonic link which lay behind the glowing praise Kennedy-Cox showered upon the Bishop of Barking in his autobiography: "We [at the Dockland Settlement] had a string of Episcopal friends. My first two were in far-off days, the very wise Bishop of St. Albans (Dr. Jacobs) and the saintly Bishop of Barking (Dr. Stevens). The first I met merely on formal occasions, the second *I met continuously in our mean little streets and upon many other occasions*, when one could learn to respect and love the simplicity of this dear old man."[35] No other mention is made of his Masonic links, although Freemasonry abounded in the East End during Kennedy-Cox's time there.

It would seem that, alongside his sense of Christian responsibility, Kennedy-Cox was highly motivated by witchcraft and Masonic practice. To what extent that impinged on his ministry in Canning Town is unclear. Whether Dockland Settlement No.1 was ever used for witchcraft activities, and to what extent fellow Settlement workers endorsed these practices, is not known. What is clear, however, is that this aspect of Kennedy-Cox's character must not be underestimated - far less overlooked - in an attempt to write an orthodox evangelical history of the development of youth work in Canning Town and at Dockland Settlement No.1.

The Youth Ministry: Pre-Great War

Exactly when Kennedy-Cox began work at the Malvern College Mission is unclear. Watherston stated that "he arrived in 1907."[36] However, the real date is likely to have been three years earlier. Commenting upon the successful development of the Mission in his autobiography, Kennedy-Cox wrote, "I had been at it just ten years and this was the summer of 1914."[37] Perhaps it is coincidence that, if 1904 is correct, his arrival would have coincided with the establishment of the Bishop of Barking Masonic Lodge.[38] Regardless of the exact date, it is certainly the case that Kennedy-Cox joined an established local team. There was *in situ* a clergyman, two lady helpers and a caretaker and his wife. Soon after his arrival, Kennedy-Cox was joined by two of his companions; the 'High-Church' Mercer and the 'Low-Church' Marquis.[39] Until 1911, Kennedy-Cox worked at the Mission on a part-time basis, continuing to live in the West End and travelling down to Canning Town three or four days a week. He did not assume personal control of the Mission until after the First World War.

His first years in Canning Town were spent establishing Boys' Clubs, his down-to-earth manner proving popular with the young people. Whenever they came to his door to play 'Knock Down Ginger', he "used to lurk behind the door and then suddenly swing it open and smack the head of the nearest child."[40] Such an informal approach won him early respect and success came quickly. The first Club was sub-divided at an early stage: the A's were the Adults, the B's were the Balmy's, the C's were the Clean and the D's were the Dirty. Before long, four Clubs for adults were also in operation and further accommodation was required.

Kennedy-Cox wasted no time in starting a football team.[41] He was always keen to organise rugged sporting activities alongside spiritual pursuits in order to maintain a holistic balance in the lives of his young people. This approach was very much in keeping with a period during which, to no small degree, imperialist fears motivated patterns of youth work.[42] The importance of physical fitness was not underestimated for a class of people who, at any given moment, may be called upon to defend their country in the face of military aggression.

Reflecting upon the social deprivation that confronted him, Kennedy-Cox "felt that the whole question was not a political problem at all but a spiritual one."[43] The question at the heart of Kennedy-Cox's philosophy was quite simple: "Were we going to attempt to give these lads any religion at all; or were we going to funk it? If we had sufficient courage to tackle the problem, what kind of religion were we going to give them?"[44] To date, there had been a Sunday Bible Class for the boys, which Kennedy-Cox realised was "a dire failure...insincere, and practically valueless."[45] He soon replaced this with a short evening service at the end of mid-week Club nights. Unconvinced that Anglo-Catholic ritualism was the answer, it was nevertheless completely in character that Kennedy-Cox should be more concerned with the environment within which acts of worship took place than the style of worship itself. He was mortified by the Mission's "poor little church" which he described as "horribly ugly."[46] He made a "solemn vow to replace it one day with a building which should directly convey to the people the beauty and majesty of the Church Militant here on earth."[47] His dream was realised in a Dedication Service for a new Chapel in March 1930, with the Queen in attendance, at a total building cost of £14,000.[48]

By 1910, there was some conflict within the Mission as to how much emphasis should be placed on evangelistic endeavour amongst young people in the local community. The Marquis was keen on pursuing a conversionist policy, whilst Mercer was concerned to nurture boys into traditional Anglicanism. Kennedy-Cox took no firm line on the style and content of evangelism.[49] What is clear, however, is that evangelistic policy was determined in competition with St. Luke's Parish Church. An example of this is in the events of 1910. At the beginning of the year, it was announced at St. Luke's that the Bishop of

St. Albans would be holding a Mission in the parish in November 1911[50] with Mr. Townsend, the Warden of the House of Mercy, Great Maplestead.[51] Such long notice period was given in order to make 1910 a year of prayer and preparation. Upon hearing the news, the Malvern College Mission decided to pre-empt the St. Luke's Mission with their own, inviting either the Cowley or the Mirfield Fathers. The Mission culminated in a 1910 Watch Night Service which filled the Chapel.[52] This activity at the Malvern College Mission forced St. Luke's to abandon their own Watch Night Service, which had traditionally been one of the highlights of the year. The reason given by St. Luke's was that New Years Eve fell on a Saturday night and there would be no value in holding a late service.[53] To be sure, that reason had affected church policy in 1904 but, on that earlier occasion, the Watch Night Service had only been brought forward from 11.30 p.m. to 7.30 p.m.[54] It is evident that St. Luke's felt unable to compete with the Malvern College Mission on this occasion and bowed to the pressure of events. There is no evidence that St. Luke's were invited to participate in, or even attend, the Malvern College Mission Watch Night Service.

In the light of the above, it is ironic that spiritual growth in the Mission only began in earnest after the 1911 appointment of Reverend Sam Tinley who, seven years later, would transfer to the incumbency of St. Luke's. Prior to that date, Tinley had been Assistant Missioner[55] but came into his own after the departure of Rev. F. A Lee[56] to the foreign mission field.[57] With great candour, Kennedy-Cox commented that, "Sam Tinley was, and is, an ideal East End Missioner. I envy him."[58] Kennedy-Cox's charismatic personality drew the crowds to the Mission and "Sam held them once they were there!"[59] Kennedy-Cox recounted that, after the appointment of Tinley, "it was success all the way; the boys at school loved their new Missioner, the West End Committees were fascinated by him, and, to my joy, I was given a free hand to do what I liked and how I liked."[60]

Tinley and Kennedy-Cox embarked on a programme of spiritual and social reform that, in the latter's own estimation began "to achieve the almost impossible, and make at least a definite impression upon a hard-bitten neighbourhood."[61] Whilst commending their missionary zeal, we must not credit them with too much originality in their methodology. The football team was matched, even outstripped, by similarly successful work at St. Luke's. Since November 1904, there had been two teams there and it was commented, "football is going strong at S. Luke's."[62] Efforts towards Temperance were likewise well established at the parish church.[63] Work amongst Dockers supplemented the well-established and sacrificial Dock Shelter ministry already offered by St. Luke's.[64] The opening of a Malvern College Mission cinema around 1912 had been pre-empted three years earlier by the Canning Town Cinematograph Hall. Indeed, by 1917, at least nineteen cinemas were open in the borough of West Ham.[65] The work of the Mission was vital and visionary but not unique. Nevertheless, success bred success and, by 1914, literally hundreds of local people were availing themselves of the facilities each week. In the twenty years of its existence, the Mission had been transformed.

Then the war came, the impact on Canning Town being immense in terms of human and economic cost. The atmosphere became one of great stress and anxiety, not helped by extensive rioting on Ascension Day 1915, during which looting caused £100,000 of damage in the West Ham district.[66] Food rationing, air-raids and an influenza epidemic claiming 1000 lives added to the difficulties. Perhaps the most devastating incident was a massive explosion at the Brunner Mond TNT factory in nearby Silvertown.[67] Seventy-three local people were killed and another four hundred seriously injured. The extent of the damage was exacerbated by the fact that the newly built Silvertown fire station was itself destroyed in the blast. The impact on local facilities cannot be fully assessed but was vast. St. Luke's Schools, for example, took the full force of the blast and the Mission Church was severely damaged too. The Treasury repudiated legal liability and offered only £557 towards repairs.[68] The Canning Town community suffered greatly during the First World War and it was the task of both Parish Church and Malvern College Mission to minister in the midst of that suffering and offer a spiritual lead.

Kennedy-Cox was aware that his action at the outbreak of war would greatly influence the young men who attended the Mission so, along with the other four male staff, he enlisted for active service in France.[69] His experiences overseas are well documented in his autobiography and need not detain us here. Details of the Mission work during his absence are understandably scant. However, enjoying a brief period of leave, Kennedy-Cox returned to the Mission only to find that "All my boys were away, all the girls making explosives, [and] it looked very grey and depressing."[70] It appears to have been a period of marking time and general pastoral support to an area devastated by human grief and incalculable loss. There had been a series of temporary Missioners during the war, all of whom served under the auspices of local part-time workers, Tom Wilson and Miss Oliver. However, "the result was that the whole place had drifted into an uncared-for state, and "the general atmosphere was such that I could not imagine any virile person desiring to come to it, as a social centre, let alone a spiritual one."[71] The youth work was largely suspended and day-to-day survival was made bearable by the hope for a future in which normality would return under the banner of freedom from fear and oppression.

The Youth Ministry: Between the Wars

Post-war society was, of course, very different from that which had been previously experienced. Class differences had become, to some extent, eroded through the creation of what Kennedy-Cox called the "temporary gentleman."[72] The few young men who returned were older and wiser. The young women who had played their part in the munitions factories had tasted the first fruits of emancipation. Society was to undergo a period of reconstruction that would effect the very fabric of its being.

Kennedy-Cox returned to the Malvern College Mission on the condition that he would assume complete control of the work. Reverend Sam Tinley transferred to the incumbency of St. Luke's and so Kennedy-Cox was left with no full-time staff and no money for the work. However, "as I had a private income, which I had scarcely touched during the War, I was able to set about collecting a paid staff."[73] Miss Oliver was recruited to head up the Women's and Girl's Work and Kennedy-Cox received a license from the Bishop to lead services. Suitable recruitment for the Boys' Clubs proved difficult until the arrival of a number of Kennedy-Cox's wartime colleagues: Harold Kimberley, Burtwell Wigmore, Wybourne Reed, Captain Ben Tinton and Captains Bromwich, Kedge and Kalberer.[74] This move towards self-contained responsibility was further strengthened by the change of name, from Malvern College Mission to Dockland Settlement. A new work demanded a new vision, one in which the young people of the area would be turned into "first-class-citizens, able to bear their share in coping with all the grave problems which were already facing post-War

England."[75] The vision was captured in the creation of an emblem for the Settlement: an Elizabethan ship, from the period when "men were men and the spirit of adventure was rife in the land."[76] Such was Kennedy-Cox's approach to the reconstruction of youth work in Canning Town.

This resurgence of youth work at the Settlement again focussed on Club activities. More Clubs than ever before were formed, each with a Canteen, serviced by a host of part-time female volunteers, many from West End society.[77] There were football clubs, swimming clubs, draughts clubs and chess clubs. The Settlement also provided Clubs where the young people could just relax and do nothing since "These young people have been so tired out by their day's work that they've not been in a fit state, not just for continued education - if they had wanted it - but even to play."[78] The girls were encouraged to take up outdoor activities to offset the negative effects of working in factories and shops throughout the day. To that end, hockey and netball were greatly encouraged. Kennedy-Cox was determined to create surroundings for his young people that would enable them to "feel exhilarated directly they enter our doors from the usually rain-sodden streets."[79] To that end, new clubrooms were systematically added to the existing buildings, the decor based on Tudor brilliance "with its heraldry and exhilarating suggestions of glorious, vivid national life."[80] Aesthetic consideration determined even the choice of chair for the boys to sit on; in the main clubroom, the same design as used for Bishops at the Athenaeum[81] and, in the canteens, "modern cocktail stools".[82] Great care was taken in providing luxurious lavatories with roller-towels and scented soap, the latter being of particular fascination to the boys![83]

Kennedy-Cox took a strategic approach in forming his Clubs; he made it a policy to "have always started with young men, rather than with small boys."[84] The rationale behind this idea was that small boys would want to be associated with the activities of older boys but the reverse would never be true. To that end, the first purchases for a club were always "a billiard table, two dart boards at least...four, six, or eight card-tables (*no* gambling) and, most important of all - a canteen...(by the way, don't forget to take out your license to sell tobacco)."[85] Each member would write his name in the attendance book and 'subs' would be collected on a Friday night.[86] Crucial to the success of the Dockland Settlement youth work was the policy that the Clubs should be open every night of the week as well as Sunday afternoons.[87] Furthermore, they would only be open for two hours per night: "How much better to have your members going home reluctant and laughing cheerily at being 'chucked out so early' and looking forward eagerly to the next evening with its set programme and swiftly passing two crowded hours!"[88]

Kennedy-Cox's pragmatism stretched to an understanding of "*the very real necessity for girls' Clubs in conjunction with boys' Clubs*, or rather the need for 'mixed Clubs'...[since] it must be obvious that growing boys and girls have to meet somewhere for social intercourse."[89] This went hand in hand with a liberal belief that it should be a youth worker's responsibility to offer sex education. Dock parents were not able to face the task, school teachers were too busy, so "it really is one of [a youth worker's] duties, providing always that it is at the parents' request, or certainly with their consent," adding that "There are so many modern beautiful books dealing with this intensely difficult subject."[90]

Kennedy-Cox also stressed that “Camps must always play a big part in the health of young industrial workers.”[91] It was a policy at the Settlement that priority should be given to camp activities and that financial support should be offered to enable most, if not all, the young people to spend at least some time away each year. Theirs was not, however, the strict regime of traditional boys’ camps. Kennedy-Cox was sympathetic to the fact that this annual break would be the only chance a young boy may have and as such “he has to crowd into these seven days, all the memories of fun and perhaps romance, with which he fills the dull winter evenings.”[92] Smart dressing and evenings spent at the cinema, on piers or in charabancs were the normal activities of these camps and romance was often high on the agenda! Predating the Mayflower’s own interest in this, Kennedy-Cox also put great energies in the 1930s into overseas holidays and camps abroad. His young people were privileged to visit France, Belgium, Switzerland, Italy and Germany.[93] In 1939, Kennedy-Cox was moved to write that these foreign holidays “give what I can only describe as ‘vision’ to the Club members, and most of us need that pretty badly in these bewildering days.”[94]

The Youth Ministry: After World War Two

There are few records available concerning the activities of Dockland Settlement No.1 during the Second World War. Canning Town, like the rest of the East End of London, suffered so severely during the air raids that we must assume much of the paperwork was destroyed.[95] Peter Watherston has detailed this period to the best of his ability in *A Different Kind of Church.*[96] In his book, he mentioned the sterling work carried out by the bursar, Reginald Logan Hunt, in maintaining the buildings. The Clubrooms were occasionally used as a mortuary and dormitories. The Residents' Hostels were used to house Irish labourers who worked as demolition gangs. The women's hostel was used for billeting army officers and those who were involved in rebuilding the docks. Again, youth work was almost completely suspended for the duration of the war. We must concur with Watherston's estimation that "The war left Dockland Settlement in a sorry state. The building had deteriorated badly and they had run into debt."[97] The impact of German bombing on an area that was built primarily on marshland was such that the chapel and hostels had become so damaged that extensive underpinning was required. Kennedy-Cox was persuaded to come back for a limited period to motivate the reconstruction but his impact, and enthusiasm for the task, was understandably limited.

The decade after cessation of conflict was a difficult and depressing time for the Settlement. Certainly, there was much activity for young people to enjoy: table tennis, cookery, pottery, lino-cutting, arts, handicrafts, beauty classes, woodwork, square dancing, swimming, boxing and an Army Cadet troop, to name but a few activities.[98] These were supplemented by regular holidays and, in 1955, a Scout Camp at Malvern. The problem lay with continuity of leadership. Miss Oliver, Miss Truscott and Douglas Minton had remained loyal to the work but establishing an authority figure proved more difficult. Harold Kimberley was Warden until his death from a brain tumour in 1953.[99] He was succeeded by Mr. MacNay who resigned in 1956, evidently discouraged by the turn of events. Three Club leaders left with him: Mr. Denton, Mrs. Mander and Mrs. Hurst. The same year, John Jones left to become Warden of a Settlement in Pimlico. Reverend David Gardner joined as Chaplain in October 1955, funded by both Malvern College and 'London over the Border'. Minton became Senior Leader but, in 1957, most of the remaining paid Club members were made redundant.

1957 was a decisive year for the Dockland Settlement. Perhaps symbolically, the Royal President, Princess Marie-Louise, missed the annual Mansion House dinner for the Settlement and died the next day. Shifting subsoil created further damage to the fabric. The rates for the property increased dramatically from an already staggering £866 per annum. The heating and lighting bill was in excess of £1000 per annum.[100] The severity of the situation could no longer be avoided and Mr. Alan Selbourne was charged with the task of disposing of the property.

On 1 August 1957, after 63 years of magnificent, sacrificial and visionary ministry in one of the toughest environments England had known, Dockland Settlement No.1 ceased to exist.

It was at that point that the Bishop of Barking came forward with a proposal for a new work. Perhaps the ministry could be salvaged and rebuilt in some different format. The Bishop knew just the man for the task - a young, energetic clergyman of some fame and international renown: England cricketer, Reverend David Sheppard. Thus began the second phase of this most influential youth work under the new name of the Mayflower Family Centre.

NOTES

[1] Kennedy-Cox, *An Autobiography*, p.41

[2] Kennedy-Cox, *An Autobiography*, p.48

[3] Kennedy-Cox, *An Autobiography*, p.47

---

[4] Kennedy-Cox, *An Autobiography*, p.87. This is, of course, a reference to the book entitled *The Wit and Wisdom of Dean Inge*, (London: Longmans, Green and Co. Ltd, 1927).

[5] Kennedy-Cox, *An Autobiography*, p.87

[6] Kennedy-Cox, *An Autobiography*, p.89f.

[7] Boyd had gone to Hertford in 1877 and remained there until 1922.

[8] Kennedy-Cox, *An Autobiography*, p.59

[9] Kennedy-Cox, *An Autobiography*, p.58

[10] Kennedy-Cox, *An Autobiography*, p.63

[11] Kennedy-Cox, *An Autobiography*, p.15

[12] Kennedy-Cox, *An Autobiography*, p.90

[13] Kennedy-Cox, *An Autobiography*, p.315

[14] Knoblock, Introduction to *An Autobiography*, p.13

[15] Knoblock, in his Introduction to Kennedy-Cox, *An Autobiography*, p.12

[16] Kennedy-Cox, *An Autobiography*, p.316

[17] Kennedy-Cox, *An Autobiography*, p.31

[18] Kennedy-Cox, *An Autobiography*, p.16f.

[19] Kennedy-Cox, *An Autobiography*, p.18

[20] Watherston, *A Different Kind of Church*, p.18

[21] Kennedy-Cox, *Through the Dock Gates*, p.33

[22] Kennedy-Cox, *An Autobiography*, p.70

[23] Kennedy-Cox, *An Autobiography*, p.71

[24] Kennedy-Cox, *Through the Dock Gates*, p.34

[25] Kennedy-Cox, *An Autobiography*, p.77

[26] Kennedy-Cox, *An Autobiography*, p.118

[27] Kennedy-Cox, *An Autobiography*, p.40

[28] Kennedy-Cox, *An Autobiography*, p.34

[29] Kennedy-Cox, *An Autobiography*, p.279ff.

[30] Kennedy-Cox, *An Autobiography*, p.41

[31] Kennedy-Cox, *An Autobiography*, p.89

[32] *Daily Telegraph* obituary for Cecil Williamson, n.d.

[33] Kennedy-Cox, *An Autobiography*, p.49

[34] www.london-lodges.org/section4.html

[35] Kennedy-Cox, *An Autobiography*, p.232 (italics mine).

[36] Watherston, *A Different Kind of Church*, p.18

[37] Kennedy-Cox, *An Autobiography*, p.140

[38] The *Malvern College Register* gives the names of the officials of the Malvern College Masonic Lodge and Kennedy-Cox held no position in that. Unless he retained membership at Oxford - and there is no record of his return there after his University days - it seems likely that he would have sought membership at least, or even a Committee position, at a local Lodge.

[39] Kennedy-Cox, *An Autobiography*, p.97

[40] Kennedy-Cox, *An Autobiography*, p.92

[41] Kennedy-Cox, *An Autobiography*, p.84

[42] B. Davies explores this issue in *From Voluntaryism to Welfare State*, (Leicester: National Youth Agency, 1999), p.10

[43] Kennedy-Cox, *Through the Dock Gates*, p.35

[44] Kennedy-Cox, *An Autobiography*, p.104

[45] Kennedy-Cox, *An Autobiography*, p.104

[46] Kennedy-Cox, *An Autobiography*, p.106

[47] Kennedy-Cox, *An Autobiography*, p.106

[48] Details of the Dedication Service were recorded in *The Express* on Saturday 5 April 1930

[49] Kennedy-Cox, *An Autobiography*, p.108

[50] *St. Luke's Parish, Victoria Docks*, news sheet, January 1910

[51] *St. Luke's Parish, Victoria Docks*, news sheet, October 1910

[52] Kennedy-Cox, *An Autobiography*, p.109

[53] *St. Luke's Parish, Victoria Docks*, news sheet, December 1910

[54] *St. Luke's Parish, Victoria Docks*, news sheet, December 1904

[55] Kennedy-Cox, *An Autobiography*, p.121

[56] *Malvern College Register*, p.xxiii

[57] Kennedy-Cox, *An Autobiography*, p.120

[58] Kennedy-Cox, *An Autobiography*, p.120

[59] Kennedy-Cox, *An Autobiography*, p.120

[60] Kennedy-Cox, *An Autobiography*, p.121

[61] Kennedy-Cox, *An Autobiography*, p.128

[62] *St. Luke's Parish, Victoria Docks*, news sheet, November 1904

[63] Details of the various Temperance Guilds were issued on each monthly issue of *St. Luke's Parish, Victoria Docks*, news sheet

[64] This work, chronicled on a regular basis in *St. Luke's Parish, Victoria Docks* monthly news sheet, offered food and shelter to Dockers throughout the Winter months, closing at Easter each year.

[65] Powell, (ed), *West Ham 1886-1986*, p.41

[66] *St. Luke's, Victoria Docks*, news sheet, June 1915

[67] Full details of this incident can be found in M. Paris, *Silvertown 1917* (Hornchurch: Ian Henry Publications, 1986)

[68] For details, see the 1917 editions of *St. Luke's, Victoria Docks*, monthly news sheets.

[69] Kennedy-Cox, *An Autobiography*, p.148

[70] Kennedy-Cox, *An Autobiography*, p.191

[71] Kennedy-Cox, *An Autobiography*, p.214

[72] Kennedy-Cox, *An Autobiography*, p.213

[73] Kennedy-Cox, *Through the Dock Gates*, p.83

[74] All bar Captain Kalberer - who died prematurely from his war wounds - continued with the Dockland Settlement movement until and beyond Kennedy-Cox's resignation in 1938.

[75] Kennedy-Cox, *An Autobiography*, p.218

[76] Kennedy-Cox, *An Autobiography*, p.226

[77] Kennedy-Cox, *Through the Dock Gates*, p.69

[78] Kennedy-Cox, *Through the Dock Gates*, p.110

[79] Kennedy-Cox, *An Autobiography*, p.245

[80] Kennedy-Cox, *An Autobiography*, p.245

[81] Kennedy-Cox, *An Autobiography*, p.245

[82] Kennedy-Cox, *Through the Dock Gates*, p.69

[83] Kennedy-Cox, *An Autobiography*, p.246

[84] Kennedy-Cox, *Through the Dock Gates*, p.57

[85] Kennedy-Cox, *Through the Dock Gates*, p.58 (italics his).

[86] Kennedy-Cox, *Through the Dock Gates*, p.60f.

[87] Kennedy-Cox, *Through the Dock Gates*, p.62

[88] Kennedy-Cox, *Through the Dock Gates*, p.63

[89] Kennedy-Cox, *Through the Dock Gates*, p.77 (italics his).

[90] Kennedy-Cox, *Through the Dock Gates*, p.100

[91] Kennedy-Cox, *Through the Dock Gates*, p.148

[92] Kennedy-Cox, *Through the Dock Gates*, p.149

[93] Kennedy-Cox, *Through the Dock Gates*, p.153

[94] Kennedy-Cox, *Through the Dock Gates*, p.154

[95] I have made extensive enquiries concerning the whereabouts of further archive material. Despite contacting two former Chairmen and a Treasurer of the Dockland Settlement movement, as well as the

relatives of another Chairman, I have, to date, been unable to locate the material.

[96] Watherston, *A Different Kind of Church*, p.30

[97] Watherston, *A Different Kind of Church*, p.30

[98] Details of these activities are recorded in *Dockland Settlement Report and Accounts, 1955-56*

[99] Watherston, *A Different Kind of Church*, p.31

[100] *The Dockland Settlement Report and Accounts, 1956-57*

Chapter Five

Assessing the Dockland Settlement Youth Ministry

In our final chapter, we now assess the youth ministry undertaken at Dockland Settlement No.1. Given the nature of our framework, it is important to undertake this task within the wider remit of *context* and *trend*, as well as *theme*. In so doing, we shall assess the work by three criteria: first, as a spiritual youth ministry, second, as an evangelical youth ministry, third, as a philanthropic youth ministry. As with the last chapter, we shall resist drawing conclusions here so that a more considered culmination of this book can immediately follow.

A Spiritual Youth Ministry

Religion was the focal point of all youth work undertaken at Dockland Settlement No.1. As Kennedy-Cox commented, "no matter how effective social work is made, unless it has a firm religious basis it leads inevitably to a *cul-de-sac*."[1] Regular services were supplemented by Sunday bicycle rides to other local, and not so local, churches. The football team had its own service before the start of each game. At one stage, Kennedy-Cox was taking up to ten services each Sunday, a demanding schedule that proved hazardous to his health.[2] However, his approach to leading young people in life of worship was both creative and visionary. None of the services lasted for more than twenty minutes in acknowledgement of the fact that levels of concentration and depths of religious fervour were somewhat limited amongst the young people. All the homilies dealt "primarily with the affairs of to-day, the things which are happening all around us and yet in some mysterious way are part of God's plan." Kennedy-Cox acknowledged that his young people were "interested neither in remote Jewish history, nor the poetry and thunder of (to them) legendary prophets."[3] His concern was to promote the truths of the faith always in a manner both accessible and relevant to youth.

As has been mentioned above, the design and creation of an aesthetically beautiful chapel was of prime importance to the Settlement vision. Based upon the Lincoln's Inn dining hall, the chapel sported an exquisitely timbered roof with an exterior leaded weathercock. Stained-glass windows threw a kaleidoscope of colour throughout, setting off pennants for the four national patron Saints, the Cenotaph flag, which had been donated by the Government, and the finely upholstered pews. Kennedy-Cox firmly believed that such surroundings of beauty would enable all worshippers to approach the Throne of Grace and comprehend something of the beauty of holiness and the beauty within.

It is important, however, to acknowledge that similar work was also thriving at St. Luke's after the Great War: perhaps not surprisingly, since Tinley and Kennedy-Cox had spent so long working together. The ethos of their approach was summarised by Tinley in 1929 thus: "In the primitive Church, it was the Christian brotherliness that attracted admiration from outsiders more than anything else. So by means of Clubs and Guilds, the Church tries to create an atmosphere of true religion that will not only make a deep impression on its members, but will accompany them in their daily lives."[4] Much of St. Luke's recreational youth work was carried out at the Boyd Institute, a quite remarkable facility for the area. In 1929, Boyd activities came under the control of Jack Townsend. There were three billiard tables in one room. Another room had an area for writing, chess, draughts, cards and other games. There was also a library. Through the Canteen was a 72-foot long Annexe with a wireless. The Annexe was used for further club activities, dances, plays and drill. The decor of the Annexe altered according to the season of the year but always "an electrical device above our heads throws ever-changing coloured rays down on to the dancers nimbly fox-trotting or engaged in the more solemn movements of the "Blues"."[5] On the nights when the Boyd Institute ran a General Recreation Club, the stage in the Annexe was transformed into a boxing-ring and the wireless area became a rifle range. The rest of the area housed cricket nets, punchballs and dartboards.

By 1929, there were a variety of activities for young boys that ran in conjunction with religious activities. The Guild of St. Nicholas met on Sundays for those aged between 8 and 11. The Guild of St.

George was divided into Junior and Senior Sections, and met twice weekly to cater for 11 to 16 year olds. The Guild of St. Michael catered for all communicants of 16 years and over. There was also a Servers' Guild, a Badminton Club, a Tennis Club, a Drum and Fife Band, the 43rd West Ham Cubs and various Football and Cricket Clubs. The girls were not neglected by St. Luke's. They were serviced by the Guilds of St. Agnes (8-11 year olds), the Good Shepherd (11-14s), St. Cecilia (under 14s), St. Faith (14-16s) and St. Margaret (16 years and over). There was also a Needlework Guild, three Girl Guides packs and two Brownie packs. The various Mission churches of St. Luke's in the area largely duplicated this dedication to youth ministry in the local community.

Evidence that the Dockland Settlement and St. Luke's ever engaged in joint activities during this period is scarce. Certainly, there may have been a competitive edge to their sporting activities. In November 1937, and probably on occasions prior to that date, the Junior (14-16 year olds) Netball teams played against each other.[6] Although the score is unknown St. Luke's almost certainly won, given the triumphant end-of-season comment that "Netball teams lose only two games in twelve (14-16 side undefeated)..."[7] The abilities of St. Luke's boys shone through in a December football match in which they beat the Dockland Settlement by an unknown margin.[8] Perhaps justice was achieved for the Settlement in the fact that the 16-18 year old Netball team tied with St. Luke's at the top of the table at season's end![9]

Nevertheless, the evidence would suggest that they were in contact with each other and generally supportive of the other's work. Canon Tinley, in January 1938, commented in his *Parochial Letter*, "We are exceedingly sorry to hear that our next door neighbour - Sir

Reginald Kennedy-Cox - is resigning his Wardenship of the Dockland Settlement. From small beginnings he has built up a perfectly-equipped Settlement, and the people of Canning Town are indeed fortunate in possessing such a wonderful centre of religious and social activities."[10]

The resignation of Kennedy-Cox, after which he desired a career in politics,[11] was indeed a bitter blow for the Dockland Settlement. During his thirty years in Canning Town, he had transformed the vision of Malvern College Mission and created an enormous youth work that had touched the lives of literally thousands. The impact of his energy and drive and charismatic personality on the local community is incalculable. To what extent the Settlement could ever thrive and develop without him was, sadly, never to be tested. The Second World War put paid to that. Nevertheless, it is undoubtedly the case that Kennedy-Cox's supremely successful youth ministry was founded on his most simplistic of strategies: "Warm hearted sympathy will…bring [young people] to the cross of Christ."[12]

An Evangelical Youth Ministry

Any attempts to locate this period of the Mayflower history within the evangelical wing of the Church have been, for some, highly contentious. Watherston, for example, has stressed the Anglo-Catholic nature of Dockland Settlement worship and the ensuing clash of ideals between 'evangelical' Chaplain David Gardner and 'unconverted' youth leader Douglas Minton.[13] He even quoted, from an unsubstantiated source, the Bishop of Barking's comment that Dockland Settlement No.1 was "the seat of Satan."[14] Watherston is surely incorrect to link this episcopal comment to condemnation of a non-evangelical stance; no Bishop would have been able to carry out an effective ministry with such partisan attitudes. If the Bishop did indeed make that comment, it is more likely that he would have been referring to Kennedy-Cox's involvement in witchcraft and freemasonry. This would be an understandable conclusion for an evangelical Bishop to reach, even if he were then bound by the ethics of confidentiality not to make clear the basis of his statement.

The truth is that, in an era during which "most of the East-end clergy had converted themselves into relieving officers,"[15] Dockland Settlement No.1 remained true to its evangelical vision of holistic self-realisation through an encounter with the living Christ. Kennedy-Cox strongly endorsed relational youth work, as we have noted above. Indeed, a considerable section of *Through the Dock Gates* stresses the need to present the Gospel in a meaningful and relevant way to young people as a means of bringing about conversion and renewal of life.[16] What is clear is that Kennedy-Cox, and the Dockland Settlement movement, represented a broader tradition of evangelicalism that attempted to develop *faith* in young people, as opposed to *ritualism*. Indeed, we note from Kennedy-Cox's words a strong sense of anti-clericalism and distrust of traditional Church practice. These are not the words of an Anglo-Catholic.

That an experience of the Gospel should underpin social activism was self-evident to Kennedy-Cox. Speaking for his contemporary philanthropist colleagues, in terms reminiscent of Samuel Barnett fifty years previously, he noted that "Without religion all that is left are the bare bones of intellectual reform, with none of that divine pity and understanding, running through the whole effort, which makes the impossible become possible, whatever cynics may think to the contrary."[17] He concluded, "*men need religion* to-day, in every land and in every heart, if we are not to commit world suicide..."[18]

Kennedy-Cox was critical of traditional expressions of faith: "the Church's message is failing because the messengers seem blind to the fact that Truth can be presented in varying form and still remain the Truth."[19] With evangelical zeal and great clarity of vision, he recognised the need to "present Our Lord as a leader of to-day, a Man of the modern world, a Man of modern sorrows, a knowledgeable living personality, accessible to all men of whatever race or creed."[20] His conclusion was that "*The Clergy have not kept pace with the intellectual progress of the people...it is the Clergy who have failed, not Christ, nor His Church.*"[21] There was a lack of sympathy for those clergy who seemed to lose heart in the face of challenging urban ministry: "*Why should they lose heart?* Theirs is a vocation, they are the bearers of a message, which the whole world is waiting for or, more accurately, is needing to-day; they are privileged to offer the nations of the earth the one solution which can solve world enmity and bring universal peace, *but do they believe that?* Or perhaps it would be more fair [sic] to say, does the man in the street feel in his heart that they believe it?"[22]

Kennedy-Cox believed that the fatherhood of God could become a living reality for all those who recognised the brotherhood of man in community living. For him, the Chapel should be the focal point of the locality since without it, "there would be not just a void, it would be as though we were organisms without hearts."[23] His evangelical zeal is summed up in these words from *Through the Dock Gates*: "I am quite certain that the world can be won for Christ, just as in different corners of the Docks, many Docklanders are being won for Him."[24]

Having located Dockland Settlement No.1 within the evangelical wing of the Church, we must be sure to note also the boundaries of that location. There are two points of interest here.

First, we have portrayed the ministry of Kennedy-Cox most certainly as crucicentric, even conversionist. However, we note Watherston's observation that, upon transfer of the project to David Sheppard, "The only commitment Sir Reginald Kennedy Cox wanted was that social clubs should be carried on in a real sense and not as excuses for 'mass conversion.'"[25] Our contention is that we can only make sense of such a demand in the light of the upsurge in *one particular expression* of evangelicalism that had culminated in the Billy Graham Crusade of 1954. The ground had been prepared for this by the 1945 Church Assembly report, *Towards the Conversion of England*. This widely debated document was to be influential in the decision of William Wand, the Bishop of London, to hold a Mission to London in 1949. Worrall noted that, "At its conclusion Wand admitted that the mission had strengthened the faithful but hardly affected those outside the Churches."[26] Nevertheless, the die was cast and Graham was invited to England by a group of evangelicals who were convinced that his style of ministry would bear fruit in the nation. Kennedy-Cox could hardly have remained unaware of Graham's Greater London Crusade, held at Harringay arena in the spring and summer of 1954. Even less could he have ignored the reality that "with the Archbishop of Canterbury and the Lord Mayor of London at the concluding meeting, and that meeting attended by 120,000 people at Wembley arena and a further 65,000 at an additional meeting at the White City, the crusade was considered a great success."[27] Perhaps the memories of Hitler Youth Rallies were too recently implanted in the mind of a man who had first-hand experience of the ravages of war. Perhaps it was for more strategic and intensely pragmatic reasons that a man who had devoted thirty years of his life to relational youthwork should find that this particular expression of evangelicalism filled him with a deep sense of unease. His concern that the Mayflower Family Centre, under the auspices of Sheppard, should not undertake similar practices may have been a logical result of his desire to protect what he believed to be *authentic evangelicalism* borne out of relational care.

Second, Kennedy-Cox's evangelicalism did not lead to an endorsement of indigenous leadership; an ecclesiological ideal that would play such a vital part in the Mayflower development under David Sheppard. In short, Kennedy-Cox did not believe that the young people should run their own youth clubs. He had some anxieties about "those intellectuals who since the War have become interested in social questions [and] maintain that the control should come from within and not from without..."[28] Indeed, he wrote vociferously against this practice, stating that "the average young worker can't run a Club efficiently for himself. It is an expert's job - not necessarily a paid expert, but one who has a gift for it - one who knows!"[29] His concern was that these young men had enough to worry about with day-to-day survival, let alone organising activities for their peers. Furthermore, most of them "by force of circumstances have not even been able to organise their own lives successfully"[30] and could not be expected to do any better with a Club.

It is interesting that the debate concerning self-governing Boys' Clubs predated Kennedy-Cox's words by some half a century. There was a clear differentiation of development between London Boys' Clubs and provincial Boys' Clubs in this regard. The London model, under the influence of Pelham, was for Clubs run by a committee elected from its members. The Manchester model, under the influence of C.E.B. Russell "would have none of these experiments in self-government by the boys."[31] This was no doubt influenced by contrasting approaches to the work itself; Russell who "believed in large Clubs, full programmes and visible results"[32] did not practise Pelham's relational model. It may be noted that the Dockland Settlement was a fusion of these two methodologies: firmly committed to relational youthwork but under the benevolent dictatorship of 'expert' leadership.

It seems, on further consideration of Dockland Settlement No.1, that two evangelical visions co-existed within the one project: one located solely in person of the Warden and his supporters, the other being located in the lives and ministry of the community workers. This is a pattern that began to emerge even as early as 1919, as a brief analysis will reveal.

Dockland Settlement No.1 was, to all intents and purposes, the creation of one man: Reginald Kennedy-Cox. As we have seen, he transformed the Malvern College Mission and created a strong and viable work through the sheer charisma and energy of his personality. However, it would be wrong to give the impression that, after the early years, Kennedy-Cox was in charge of the *practicalities* of youth work at the Dockland Settlement. He remained the visionary and leader of the overall project but took an increasingly managerial and distant role.

Kennedy-Cox was an extraordinarily busy man. The Settlement he built in Canning Town was merely the first in an extensive movement that developed under his expertise. By 1930, Kennedy-Cox had opened a number of other Settlements: "No. 2", initially under the Sub-Wardenship of Kimberley, opened in the Isle of Dogs; "No. 3" opened in Bristol, the Sub-Warden being Mr. Wigmore; "No. 4" opened at Rotherhithe, the Sub-Wardens post being shared by Captain Bromwich and Miss Teesdale. "No. 5" opened in Southampton under the guidance of Mr. Stephenson.[33] Kennedy-Cox was a regular visitor to all five Settlements, although he was to admit in 1939, "I know 'No.

4' better almost than any of the other of our branches. Each week I meet the members in our chapel there..."[34]

Those extra Settlements were not the only activities to take Kennedy-Cox away from his work at the "No. 1" Settlement in Canning Town. The range of his responsibilities elsewhere is nothing short of extraordinary. For many years, Kennedy-Cox was President and Chairman of the Children's Hospital in Plaistow and the Sunshine Home in Shoeburyness.[35] His concerns, in these roles, were for the health and well-being of Dock children, most especially those with speech and hearing impediments. The Benevolent Fund, which he set up, enabled many families to enjoy a holiday at the seaside free of charge. He was also Chairman of the local committee for the Employment Exchange, a role in which he became "intensely sad, as I am forced to witness this unceasing waste of splendid human material."[36] At the other end of the age spectrum, Kennedy-Cox had real concerns for, and political involvement in, the increase of pension allowances.[37]

However, the bulk of his extra-Settlement workload was in the arena of juvenile crime and disorder. Kennedy-Cox spent many hours visiting the homes of the accused, as well as making numerous Court appearances, as a Prisoners' Friend.[38] Soon after beginning this ministry, he was appointed by the Home Office to be an official Borstal "Visitor" for two institutions and then, in the 1930s, became a Justice of the Peace for Essex, serving at Stratford in East London. He was soon elected Chairman of the Juvenile Court and Chairman of the Probation Committee, as well as being a member of the Clarke Hall Fellowship.[39] It was in recognition of such unstinting and sacrificial work that Kennedy-Cox became Sir Reginald in 1939.

Given this quantity of work and responsibility, it is hardly surprising that Kennedy-Cox should have relinquished the day-to-day running of youthwork at the Dockland Settlement. This transfer of responsibility began as early as 1919 with the arrival of Douglas 'Minnie' Minton. Arriving unannounced at the Settlement in bowler hat and carrying an ornate walking-stick, this young man from Birmingham made an immediate impression on both Kennedy-Cox and the young people of Canning Town. Twenty years later, Kennedy-Cox wrote that "Douglas Minton has a flair for clubs; he has that genius which is built upon an infinite capacity for taking pains. As director of all the clubs at "No. 1" he already has the great pleasure of seeing his younger boys growing up into young men."[40] That personal pleasure of seeing young men reaching Christian maturity would last until his retirement in 1961.

It is in the persons of Kennedy-Cox and Minton that we find represented the two evangelical visions at work at Dockland Settlement No.1. Kennedy-Cox was the great visionary, the charismatic personality, the dynamic leader. Only Kennedy-Cox could have transformed the Malvern College Mission as he did. Only Kennedy-Cox could have instilled the spiritual base and strategy for his around which he could unite his co-workers. Crucially, only Kennedy-Cox could have raised the hundreds of thousands of pounds with which to build his Settlement movement. In a very real sense, those who gave money felt they were giving to Kennedy-Cox. It was his charismatic personality that drew the support of nobility. Minton embodied the more localised model of evangelicalism. Coming from a working-class background himself, growing up as an orphan at the Queen Victoria Orphanage in Paddington, he was able to identify with the needs and aspirations of the young people. It was Minton who, night after night, would be at the Clubs, building long-lasting relationships. It was

Minton who tolerated the high jinx of the young people as well as catering for nearly one thousand people at the Settlement on a Saturday night.[41] After his late conversion, it was Minton who spent hours at the local Rathbone Market, proclaiming the Gospel and inviting young boys to his Clubs. Upon Kennedy-Cox's resignation, Minton's ministry was able to continue because it was localised and low-key and not reliant on outside support. This intensely relational youth work strategy, although epitomised by Minton, was not located solely in him. His example was to serve as an encouragement to others who sought to minister at the Settlement. Watherston lists just some of these: "Margaret Fish came as lady worker taking over the responsibility for the mums' and other ladies' clubs and for helping in the children's church on Sunday mornings. Tony Dines arrived and did much work in the Senior Boys' Club. John Lywood and Owen Jones came ...Richard Thomson, another old Malvernian, then an army captain...became a firm friend and visited frequently at weekends."[42] This dedication to relational evangelical strategy had been the hallmark of the Dockland Settlement youth ministry and would continue to epitomise the future work at the Mayflower Family Centre.

A Philanthropic Youth Ministry

It was suggested in the *Introduction* that Dockland Settlement No.1, and the Mayflower Family Centre that followed, have always been immensely privileged youth projects. The truth of that is evident in our consideration of Kennedy-Cox's tenure as Warden. The financial support offered by Malvern College was enormous, whilst the circumstances of Kennedy-Cox's own upbringing and education were completely alien to anything known by the Canning Town locals. That, however, was just the tip of the iceberg. Detailed analysis of sources of funding and patronage reveal a degree of support that could never have been generated, far less sustained, by the local Canning Town community itself.

The stark reality is that Reginald Kennedy-Cox was a genius when it came to fund-raising. He was acutely aware, from the moment that he assumed control in 1919, that "as a charitable institution we must have direct patronage."[43] The most influential form of patronage would be from the Royal Family, and it is that which Kennedy-Cox strenuously sought in the person of Princess Helena Victoria. She was already involved in developing the girls' work of the YMCA and readily agreed to become First President of the Dockland Settlement. Thereafter, Kennedy-Cox was able to win financial support from a staggering array of Royalty, nobles, lords and political benefactors: Mrs. Cyril Ward, Lord Knutsford, Lord Ritchie, Lord and Lady Astor, Lady Louis Mountbatten, the Duchess of Westminster, Lord Beattie, Lord Crewe, Lord Ebbisham, Sir Kynaston Studd, Stanley Baldwin, the list goes on and on.[44] Furthermore, the Duke of York became the Patron, making regular visits and presenting a football cup. His involvement with the youth work grew to such an extent that six Settlement boys were invited to his wedding at Westminster Abbey.[45] Princess Mary opened work on the Dockland garden. There were even visits from the King and Queen, notably for the dedication of the new Chapel.[46] Kennedy-Cox commented that "King George V, assisted by Queen Mary, was inspired with a very real understanding of the working lives of even the least conspicuous of his people, this understanding being based upon personal knowledge and direct contact."[47]

Perhaps the most regular source of income for the Dockland Settlement movement was the annual luncheon, held at the Mansion House. The benefit of such occasions was that they "afforded us a unique opportunity of putting before the city of London and the general public our ideals, methods and gradual progress." This luncheon was not unique to the Dockland Settlement, nor was it a new idea. Even as early as January 1891, there had been a similar occasion to raise £12,000 for the Oxford Settlement in Bethnal Green.[48] However, the genius of Kennedy-Cox in winning sympathy for his cause was in inviting along a number of young Settlement boys to dine with the guests. In that way, the work could be presented in more than just abstract detail to the dignitaries. Kennedy-Cox readily admitted that "These Mansion House dinners have brought into our coffers thousands of pounds."[49] It is certainly the case that Kennedy-Cox was aggressive in his fund-raising methods at these functions. One gentleman who was present at a number of these annual events told me that Kennedy-Cox had cheques and pens neatly laid beside each place-sitting at the tables!

Kennedy-Cox did not limit his fundraising activities to Britain. Perhaps acting on the advice of the fortune-teller all those years previously, he decided to spend a considerable period of time in the 1920s seeking support in America. This was not such an opportunistic venture as one might imagine since the Settlement movement was a well-established phenomenon in America by the turn of the nineteenth-century. Young and Ashton suggest that "In the United States at least four were started by persons who had their direct inspiration from English Settlements (e.g. Hull House, established by Jane Addams in Chicago, the Neighbourhood Guild in New York started by Stanton Coit in 1886, North Western University Settlement in Chicago, and South End House founded by Robert A. Woods in 1892)."[50] It is not surprising that Kennedy-Cox should have concentrated his fund-raising efforts in Chicago. He found time to visit Hull House, which, contrary to Young and Ashton's suggestion, was founded not by the celebrated Addams but two philanthropic women in September 1889. Thereafter, Addams assumed the role of Warden[51] and, after sharing a dinner with her, Kennedy-Cox declared her to be "the doyen of all Wardens."[52]

Thus, when Kennedy-Cox resigned his Wardenship in 1939, it was inevitable that support for the Dockland Settlement project would decline. His resignation was not the only reason for declining interest, of course. The creation of the Welfare State led many to believe that the need for such charitable support of those growing up in impoverished areas was now the work of Government. Furthermore, Section 53 of the 1944 Education Act strengthened state responsibility for the provision and financing of youthwork.[53] Dockland Settlement No.1 was not to regain its kudos until the arrival of the famous David Sheppard, after which the cycle was destined to repeat itself once again.

Conclusion

Resisting the temptation to anticipate our main *Conclusion*, we note at this point only to what extent many previous commentators have misunderstood Dockland Settlement No.1. We remind ourselves of David Sheppard's suggestion that its evangelical vision was "a complete failure". We remind ourselves, too, of Watherston's refusal even to locate its ministry within the evangelical wing of the church. With the greatest respect to these men, both of whom were Wardens of the Mayflower Family Centre, it may be argued that they were too close to the project and had too much of a vested interest to be entirely objective. Evidently, Kennedy-Cox was supremely concerned to provide a spiritual base for the work. His concern was primarily evangelical in that he longed for lives to be changed and for the local community to be transformed and recognised the necessity for the power of God to be at work for that to happen. He was also concerned to promote the Dockland Settlement movement on a grand, even global, stage.

In summary, Dockland Settlement No.1 was as spiritual, evangelical and immensely privileged a youth work project as the East End of London had ever seen.

NOTES

[1] Kennedy-Cox, *An Autobiography*, p.313

[2] Kennedy-Cox, *An Autobiography*, p.229

[3] Kennedy-Cox, *Through the Dock Gates*, p.230

[4] *The Journal of St. Luke's Church*, May 1929, n.p.

[5] *The Journal of St. Luke's Church*, May 1929, n.p.

[6] There was a *Fixture Notice* for the teams to meet on 13 November 1937 on the St. Luke's pitch. *The Journal of St. Luke's Church*, November 1937, n.p.

[7] *The Journal of St. Luke's Church*, December 1937, n.p.

[8] *The Journal of St. Luke's Church*, January 1938, n.p.

[9] *The Journal of St. Luke's Church*, May 1938, n.p.

[10] *The Journal of St. Luke's Church*, January 1938, n.p.

[11] Kennedy-Cox, *Through the Dock Gates*, p.11. It is difficult to ascertain whether the war thwarted his ambitions. However, it is likely that he planned to stand as a candidate for Bermondsey (see his comments on p.44 and p.254).

[12] Kennedy-Cox, *Through the Dock Gates*, p.231

[13] Watherston, *A Different Kind of Church*, p.34

[14] Watherston, *A Different Kind of Church*, p.33

[15] Eagar, *Making Men*, p.29

[16] Kennedy-Cox, *Through the Dock Gates*, p.221-234

[17] Kennedy-Cox, *Through the Dock Gates*, p.221

[18] Kennedy-Cox, *Through the Dock Gates*, p.226 (italics his).

[19] Kennedy-Cox, *Through the Dock Gates*, p.222

[20] Kennedy-Cox, *Through the Dock Gates*, p.230

[21] Kennedy-Cox, *Through the Dock Gates*, p.224 (italics his).

[22] Kennedy-Cox, *Through the Dock Gates*, p.225 (italics his).

[23] Kennedy-Cox, *Through the Dock Gates*, p.228

[24] Kennedy-Cox, *Through the Dock Gates*, p.232

[25] Watherston, *A Different Kind of Church*, p.31

[26] B.G. Worrall, *The Making of the Modern Church*, (London: SPCK, 1988), p.273

[27] Worrall, *The Making of the Modern Church*, p.274

[28] Kennedy-Cox, *Through the Dock Gates*, p.47

[29] Kennedy-Cox, *Through the Dock Gates*, p.47

[30] Kennedy-Cox, *Through the Dock Gates*, p.48

[31] A.F. Young and E.T. Ashton, *British Social Work in the Nineteenth Century*, (London: Routledge and Kegan Paul, 1956), p.255

[32] Eagar, *Making Men*, p.267

[33] Details of these are given by Kennedy-Cox in *An Autobiography*, p.253f. Further Dockland Settlements were opened, bringing the total number to nine. However, without extant archives, it is difficult to assess exactly how much Kennedy-Cox was involved in the creation of the latter projects. In all likelihood, they opened after his retirement.

[34] Kennedy-Cox, *An Autobiography*, p.256

[35] Kennedy-Cox, *Through the Dock Gates*, p.138

[36] Kennedy-Cox, *Through the Dock Gates*, p.205

[37] Kennedy-Cox, *Through the Dock Gates*, p.254

[38] Kennedy-Cox, *Through the Dock Gates*, p.190

[39] Kennedy-Cox, *Through the Dock Gates*, p.195

[40] Kennedy-Cox, *An Autobiography*, p.257

[41] His reflections are recorded in *The Log of the Mayflower*, Winter 1961

[42] Watherston, *A Different Kind of Church*, p.38

[43] Kennedy-Cox, *An Autobiography*, p.220

[44] For details of these benefactors and their particular involvement, see Kennedy-Cox, *An Autobiography, passim*

[45] Kennedy-Cox, *An Autobiography*, p.225

[46] For details of their first visit see Kennedy-Cox, *An Autobiography*, p.246f. For the Queen's attendance at the Chapel service, see the same source, p.306f.

[47] Kennedy-Cox, *Through the Dock Gates*, p.71

[48] Eagar, *Making Men*, p.202

[49] Kennedy-Cox, *An Autobiography*, p.238

[50] Young and Ashton, *British Social Work in the Nineteenth Century*, p.232

[51] For Adams' views on the Settlement movement, especially in relation to the Hull House work, see her lecture "The Subjective Necessity for Social Settlements," given to the Ethical Culture Societies in 1892, in J. Addams, *Philanthropy and Social Progress*, (New York: Thomas Y. Crowell & Co., 1893), p.1-26

[52] Kennedy-Cox, *An Autobiography*, p.288

[53] For details, see Davies, *From Voluntaryism to the Welfare State*, p.21f.

Conclusion

Writing of the period when many of these great Boys' Clubs, Institutes, Missions and Settlements were founded, Eagar rightly commented, "That was the heroic age, but the heroes had no inkling of it."[1] There is an unhealthy arrogance in those who snipe at the attainments of these Victorian gentleman and their efforts for social and spiritual reform. To accuse them of self-righteousness and attitudes of superiority is to present a desperately cruel and inaccurate caricature. Eagar defended these men by assuring the reader that "...personal service in the Victorian slums was a rigorous affair. It did not attract the weaklings, the snobs or the self-indulgent."[2] It is conspicuous, though perhaps not surprising, that ex-soldiers played an enormous role in the formation of youth work for boys in Great Britain. General Gordon devoted himself to boys' work at Gravesend. The work of General

Baden-Powell has achieved even greater renown. We have noted the direction of Dockland Settlement No.1 under the leadership of Kennedy-Cox and his army pals. As Eagar astutely commented, "These men were not concerned with man-power so much as with manhood," focussing on the development of such virtues as loyalty, courage, endurance and discipline.[3]

Yet it is most certainly the case that youth work in the late-nineteenth-century, not least in East London, was predominantly motivated by religious idealism. In their book, *British Social Work in the Nineteenth Century*, Young and Ashton suggested that only the Co-operative Youth Clubs and Army Cadets were founded without a primarily religious motivation "and even these were never indifferent to Christianity."[4] Regardless of churchmanship, there was an evangelical fervour to the work of promoting Christian knowledge and the leading of young men and women to a transformative experience of the crucified Christ. That religious zeal was only supplemented in the first half of the twentieth-century with an emphasis on social education and the promotion of holistic maturity.

Although the need for brevity has prevented us from providing little more than a snapshot of the evolution of urban youth ministry from 1880-1957, clear patterns have emerged. We shall conclude our study by briefly drawing attention to three of these.

First, we note the pivotal importance of charismatic leadership in developing successful urban youth ministry. Kennedy-Cox has provided the most exceptional example of that. Had we been so minded, we could have explored the ministry of others: Pelham, Russell, Ferguson, Carter – a dozen or more successful urban youth practitioners developed their ministry during this period reliant primarily on magnetic and energetic personality traits. The question raised by this thesis is whether or not urban youth projects developed under charismatic leadership can ever survive after the founder has moved on. The experience of Dockland Settlement No.1, along with many of the Public School Missions from this period, suggests that they cannot – at least, in their original format. Indeed, subsequent Mayflower Family Centre history – under the Wardenships of Revds. David Sheppard, Denis Downham and Roger Sainsbury – suggests that this is a lesson they were unable, or unwilling, to learn at all. The longevity of urban youth ministry has been much the poorer for that lack of clarity.

Second, we note the fundamental importance of philanthropic support and related profiling of youth projects. Again, Dockland Settlement No.1 provides us with the perfect example of how utterly reliant many urban youth projects during our period were on external funding and support. McG. Eagar's book, *Making Men*, tells a similar story for numerous other works. The question raised by this thesis is whether it is appropriate to 'impose' a magnificent project on a local community or whether youth ministry should be primarily indigenous, growing out of – and reflecting – the locality. Is it possible for a community to 'own' such a work as Dockland Settlement No.1 or does it further serve to pauperise an area? Certainly, such a grand project could never have been achieved through local support alone. To be sure, there are many in Canning Town who still have fond memories of their time at the Settlement. However, it is undoubtedly the case that they are grateful for a 'project provided' rather than proud of a 'ministry grown'. Whilst one may not be superior to the other, we note the fundamental difference between the two.

Third, and finally, we note the underlying strategy of relational youth work as a primary model for successful urban youth ministry during our period. Whilst acknowledging that the term 'relational youth work' is often over-used and misunderstood – and resisting the temptation to define it at this late stage – we note only that relational care is a Gospel quality not a personal commodity. Dockland Settlement No.1, and many of the other projects mentioned in this work, prove that youth ministry need not be caught in a dichotomy between big/impersonal and small/relational. Underpinned by an appropriate spiritual vision that informs all practice, it is possible to develop a large work that retains a relational methodology and objective.

Finally, we refer once more to Checkland in *The Study of Urban History*: "All urban historians should be concerned with trend, theme, and context. But for progress to be made there is need for some degree of concentration of effort…Indeed, in the present state of affairs, those who make thumping generalisations about what happened…are likely to find themselves highly vulnerable."[5]

It is to be hoped that we have avoided the temptation to make 'thumping generalisations' which would only serve to make the thesis vulnerable. By carefully moving through an objective study of *context* and *trend*, we have then been able to concentrate effort on our *theme*. In so doing, we have uncovered a most exciting story of creative and energetic youth ministry in East London. Most important, it is a story from which all of us who are youth practitioners have much to learn. It is to be hoped that real progress has been made in this field of study and that others will be encouraged to make further inroads for the benefit of the Church and those amongst whom we minister.

NOTES

[1] Eagar, *Making Men*, p.208

[2] Eagar, *Making Men*, p.225

[3] Eagar, *Making Men*, p.97

[4] Young and Ashton, *British Social Work in the Nineteenth Century*, p.253

[5] Checkland, *The Study of Urban History*, p.359

BIBLIOGRAPHY AND SOURCES

As mentioned in the Introduction, literally hundreds of primary source papers, microfiches and other records have been accessed during the research of this paper. For the sake of brevity, only those referred to in the text have been listed here.

PRIMARY SOURCES

Barnett, S.A., 'Settlements of university men in great towns. A paper read at St John's, Oxford on 17th November 1883', Oxford: The Chronicle Company. Reprinted in J. Pimlott, *Toynbee Hall. Fifty years of social progress 1884 - 1934*, (London: J. M. Dent, 1935)

Dickens, C., 'Londoners Over the Border', *Household Words*, No.390, Saturday September 12, 1857, n.p.

Dockland Settlement, *Docklands Settlement Report and*

Accounts, 1955-56

---, *Docklands Settlement Report and Accounts, 1956-57*

Hertford College, extant papers relating to the life and work of Dr. Henry Boyd

Mayflower, *The Log of the Mayflower*, Spring 1960

---, *The Log of the Mayflower*, Winter 1961

Poor Law Commissioners, *Chadwick Report*, 'From the Poor Law Commissioners on an Inquiry into the Sanitary Conditions of the Labouring Population of Great Britain,' London, 1842

Salmon, H.G.C. (ed.), *Malvern College Register 1865-1924*, (London: Charles Murray, 1925)

St. Luke's, Victoria Docks, *St. Luke's Parish, Victoria Docks*, news sheet, November 1904

---, *St. Luke's Parish, Victoria Docks*, news sheet, December 1904

---, *St. Luke's Parish, Victoria Docks*, news sheet, January 1910

---, *St. Luke's Parish, Victoria Docks*, news sheet, October 1910

---, *St. Luke's Parish, Victoria Docks*, news sheet, December 1910

---, *St. Luke's Parish, Victoria Docks*, news sheet, June 1915

---, *St. Luke's Parish, Victoria Docks*, news sheet, January 1917

---, *St. Luke's Parish, Victoria Docks*, news sheet, February 1917

---, *St. Luke's Parish, Victoria Docks*, news sheet, March 1917

---, *St. Luke's Parish, Victoria Docks*, news sheet, May 1917

---, *St. Luke's Parish, Victoria Docks*, news sheet, June 1917

---, *St. Luke's Parish, Victoria Docks*, news sheet, September 1917

---, *St. Luke's Parish, Victoria Docks*, news sheet, November 1917

---, *St. Luke's Parish, Victoria Docks*, news sheet, December 1917

---, *The Journal of St. Luke's Church*, May 1929

---, *The Journal of St. Luke's Church*, November 1937

---, *The Journal of St. Luke's Church*, December 1937

---, *The Journal of St. Luke's Church*, January 1938

---, *The Journal of St. Luke's Church*, May 1938

The Essex Review, i.68-9, n.d., n.p.

SECONDARY SOURCES

Addams, J., *Philanthropy and Social Progress*, (New York: Thomas Y. Crowell & Co., 1893)

Barnett, H., *Canon Barnett*, Vol. 1, (London: John Murray, 1918)

Barrett, G., *Blackfriars Settlement. A short history 1887 - 1987*, (London: Blackfriars Settlement, 1985)

Briggs, A., *Victorian Cities,* (Harmondsworth: Penguin, 1968)

Brooks, T., *Apples of Gold*, 1660, in *The Works of Thomas Brooks*, (Edinburgh: Banner of Truth, 1980)

Burton, G., *People Matter More Than Things*, (London: Hodder and Stoughton, 1965)

Daunton, M.J., *House and Home in the Victorian City,* (London: Edward Arnold, 1983)

Davies, B., *From Voluntaryism to Welfare State*, (Leicester: National Youth Agency, 1999)

Dickens, C., (compiler), *One Dinner a Week and Travels in the East*, articles from 'All the Year Round', (London: London Cottage Mission, 1884).

Dyos, H.J., *The Study of Urban History,* (London: Edward Arnold,

1968)

Dyos, H.J. and Wolff, M., *The Victorian City Vol.1*, (London: Routledge & Kegan Paul, 1976)

Eagar, W. McG., *Making Men*, (London: University of London Press 1953)

Fishman, W.J., *East End 1888*, (London: Duckworth, 1988)

Foulkes, R. (ed.), *British Theatre in the 1890s,* (Cambridge: Cambridge University Press, 1992)

Hanks, G., *God's Special Army: The Story of William Booth*, (Exeter: Religious Education Press, 1980)

Hattersley, R., *Blood and Fire: The Story of William and Catherine Booth and their Salvation Army*, (London: Little, Brown, 1999)

Hewitt, D and J., *George Burton - A Study in Contradictions,* (London: Hodder and Stoughton, 1969)

Howarth, E.G., & Wilson, M. (compilers), *West Ham - A Study in Social and Industrial Problems*, (London: J.M. Dent, 1907)

Kellett, J.R., *The Impact of Railways on Victorian Cities,* (London: Routledge & Kegan Paul, 1969)

Kennedy-Cox, R., *An Autobiography,* (London: Hodder and Stoughton, 1931)

---, *Through the Dock Gates,* (London: Michael Joseph Ltd., 1939)

Marchant, J. (ed.), *The Wit and Wisdom of Dean Inge*, (London: Longmans, Green and Co. Ltd, 1927).

Margetson, S., *Leisure and Pleasure in the Nineteenth Century,* (London: Cassell, 1969)

Nicoll, A., *A History of English Drama 1660-1900, vol. V,* (Cambridge: Cambridge University Press, 1946)

Noll, M.A., Bebbington, D.W., & Rawlk, G.A. (eds), *Evangelicalism*, (Oxford, 1994)

O'Neill, G., *My East End,* (Harmondsworth: Penguin, 2000)

Paris, M., *Silvertown 1917,* (Hornchurch: Ian Henry Publications, 1986)

Pelham, T., *Handbook to Youths' Institutes and Working Boys' Clubs*, (London, 1889)

Pfautz, H.W. (ed.), *Charles Booth on the City,* (Chicago: University of Chicago, 1967)

Pimlott, J., *Toynbee Hall. Fifty years of social progress 1884 – 1934*, (London: J. M. Dent, 1935)

Powell, J., *The Man Who Didn't Go to China*, (London: Lutterworth, 1947)

Powell, W.R., *Victoria Histories of the County of Essex*, (Oxford: OUP, 1973)

---, (ed.), *West Ham 1886-1986,* (Council of the London Borough of Newham, London: Plaistow Press, 1986)

Reason, W., (ed.) *University and Social Settlements*, (London: Methuen, 1898)

Roberts, D., *Victorian Origins of the British Welfare State,* (Yale: Archon Books, 1969)

Russell, J. *History of the Tate Institute, 1887-1933*, (TS 1951)

Sheppard, D., *Parson's Pitch*, (London: Hodder and Stoughton, 1964)

---, *Built as a City*, (London: Hodder and Stoughton, 1974)

Stedman Jones, G., *Outcast London,* (Oxford: Clarendon, 1971)

Thorne, G., *The Great Acceptance: The Life Story of F.N. Charrington*, (London: Hodder & Stoughton, 1913)

Tinton, B., *War Comes to the Docks*, (London: Marshall, Morgan and Scott, 1941)

Vicinus, M., *Independent Women. Work and community for single women 1850-1920,* (London: Virago, 1985)

Wagner, G., *Barnardo,* (London: Weidenfeld & Nicolson, 1979)

Ward, P., *Growing Up Evangelical,* (London: SPCK, 1996)

Watherston, P., *A Different Kind of Church,* (London: Marshall Pickering, 1994)

Williams, A.E., *Barnardo of Stepney,* (London: Allen & Unwin, 1966)

Wilson, P., *Gutter Feelings,* (London: Marshalls, 1985)

Worrall, B.G., *The Making of the Modern Church*, (London: SPCK, 1988)

Young, A.F., and Ashton, E.T., *British Social Work in the Nineteenth Century*, (London: Routledge and Kegan Paul, 1956)

NEWSPAPERS

The Stratford Express, 22 March 1913

The Express, Saturday 5 April 1930

Daily Telegraph, obituary for Cecil Williamson, n.d., n.p.

PUBLIC RECORDS

1891 Census, Public Records Office, Microfiche Reference RG12/1322

INTERVIEWS AND DETAILED CONVERSATIONS/CONTACTS

Allan Craig, current Centre Director of the Mayflower

Rita Dennis, teenager at Dockland Settlement No.1 and Mayflower

Sir Simon Hornby, former Chairman of the Dockland Settlement movement

Chris Miller, former youth worker in Canning Town and Custom House

Kate Moorhouse, Mayflower archivist

Rev. John Oliver, former youth worker at the Mayflower

Grace Raggett, teenager at Dockland Settlement No.1

Norman Rosser, archivist at Malvern College

Rt. Revd. David Sheppard, former Warden of the Mayflower

Rt. Revd. R. Sainsbury, former Warden of the Mayflower,

Rev. Dave Wade, Mayflower Council

Rev. Peter Watherston, ex-Warden of the Mayflower

WEBSITES

www.landow.stg.brown.edu/victorian

www.london-lodges.org/section4.html

Other Titles by Steve Griffiths

Redeem the Time: The Problem of Sin in the Writings of John Owen

John Owen is arguably the greatest theologian England has ever had. As Chaplain to Oliver Cromwell and father of the Congregational Church, his impact on doctrine and ecclesiology has far outlived his 17th-century context. At the heart of his writings is the doctrine of sin, which impacted not just church but nation too. As the church seeks a way forward in the 21st-century, we have much to learn from Owen.

God of the Valley: A Journey through Grief

Beginning with the toughest question of all – why? – this book is written from the author's own experience of grief, through the illness and eventual death of his wife at the age of 36, and also through his pastoral work as a church minister with bereaved families. Interwoven with his personal story are reflections on Bible passages that over the years have come to mean most to him.

Other Titles by Steve G[illegible]

[illegible]

www.ingramcontent.com/pod-product-compliance
Ingram Content Group UK Ltd.
Pitfield, Milton Keynes, MK11 3LW, UK
UKHW012232240726
13966UKWH00003B/1064